THE CON

THE CON

**How Scams Work,
Why You're Vulnerable,
and How to Protect Yourself**

James Munton and Jelita McLeod

ROWMAN & LITTLEFIELD PUBLISHERS, INC.
Lanham • Boulder • New York • Toronto • Plymouth, UK

Published by Rowman & Littlefield Publishers, Inc.
A wholly owned subsidiary of The Rowman & Littlefield Publishing Group, Inc.
4501 Forbes Boulevard, Suite 200, Lanham, Maryland 20706
http://www.rowmanlittlefield.com

Estover Road, Plymouth PL6 7PY, United Kingdom

British Library Cataloguing in Publication Information Available

Library of Congress Cataloging-in-Publication Data
Munton, James, 1971–
  The con : how scams work, why you're vulnerable, and how to protect
yourself / James Munton and Jelita McLeod.
      p. cm.
  Includes index.
  ISBN 978-1-4422-0731-8 (cloth : alk. paper) — ISBN 978-1-4422-0733-2
(electronic)
  1. Fraud—Prevention. 2. Swindlers and swindling. I. McLeod, Jelita,
1971– II. Title.
  HV6691.M86 2011
  362.88—dc22   2011008097

∞™ The paper used in this publication meets the minimum requirements of
American National Standard for Information Sciences—Permanence of Paper
for Printed Library Materials, ANSI/NISO Z39.48-1992.

Printed in the United States of America

CONTENTS

ACKNOWLEDGMENTS

Each story in this book represents an untold number of victims. These experiences, though extraordinarily painful, will serve to help many more, and we are appreciative to the individuals represented within. We are grateful to all those whose contributions helped make this book possible. David Fugate of Launch Books was instrumental in shaping the book from the outset with his guidance and insight. Special thanks to Detective Michael B. Dana, who gave generously of his time and expertise and who continues to fight the good fight against swindlers and con artists. Thank you also to Glenn Hester, another law enforcement comrade, and security specialist Marta Zaricznyj, who provided us with extremely helpful feedback. Julie Dimmick was there for us before the book was even written, and her professional and personal perspectives were invaluable throughout the process. Alex Mitchell read an early draft of the book, and his comments motivated and energized us. Thanks go to Helen Chang, Sandra Park, and Ircka West for allowing us to tap their brains and/or call upon their services. Above all, we thank our families, whose love, patience, advice, and support sustain us.

(1)

SCAMS 101

Admitting There's a Problem

"**W**hen I tell you that it started with a glass of wine at a Christmas party, you may think you know where the story's going. I can tell you for a fact that you're wrong."

Scott had a good working relationship with his boss, Nick, who was also owner and founder of the company where they worked. The two men were close in age and agreed on most aspects of the business. Scott never doubted that Nick was a talented entrepreneur and straight shooter.

"We work in a small office," says Scott. "Nick decided to have the company holiday party at his place. He had this neat bachelor pad in the city. During the party, I spilled a little wine on my shirt and I wanted to clean up, so I went into the bathroom. I looked around to see if I could find something to dab my shirt with. There was a cabinet with towels and washcloths on one shelf, and on the second, higher shelf was a collection of prescription bottles. And it really was a collection, maybe 20 or 30 bottles. I was taken aback, because I'd never known Nick to be sick. I did think it was a lot of medicine, but I also thought it was none of my business. As I was about to close the door, I took one more look up there and something caught my eye."

Scott thought he saw something familiar on one of the pill bottles. To satisfy his curiosity, he took it down and was stunned to find his own name on the label.

"It was very, very weird. The prescription was for Vicodin, which I've never taken. I grabbed another bottle. It had some other person's name on it, not Nick's. It was also for Vicodin. I ended up taking them all down. I found seven bottles with my name on them. There were prescriptions for Xanax, OxyContin, and other things I'd never heard of. I didn't know what to think. It didn't make any sense to me. Obviously there was something screwy going on, but I still didn't get why or how he would have these prescriptions in my name. So I looked at the name of the pharmacy on one of the bottles and decided to ask the pharmacist there. Then I put everything back on the shelf, went back out to the party, and tried to act normal."

What Scott discovered when he visited the pharmacy the next day was that someone, presumably Nick, had been filling prescriptions in his name for over a year. Scott contacted his insurance company, which verified that the prescriptions had been processed through his insurance policy. At first, Scott didn't know what to do with this information.

"I was completely blindsided. It was just such an odd thing to happen. I always liked Nick. He was a good boss. Obviously he had some kind of problem, and he had appropriated my identity to get these pills, which was without a doubt illegal and definitely immoral. But if I turned him in to the police, what would it mean for my job? He was not only my boss; he was the owner of the company."

Scott discussed the dilemma with his wife, who advised him to call the police. Instead, Scott decided to try confronting Nick first, thinking that if his boss was abusing drugs, the discussion might serve as a wake-up call.

"Nick tried pleading ignorance at first, but I had seen the evidence with my own eyes. Then he began to get emotional. He was all teary eyed and apologetic, said it was all a big mistake, promised he would never do it again. I took him at his word."

Scott thought he and Nick had come to an acceptable resolution. His job and the company were unaffected. When Scott went back to the insurance company, though, he found clearing up the confusion more difficult than he had anticipated. As far as the insurance company was concerned, Scott had been prescribed and had purchased the drugs in question. Without a written admission from Nick that he had stolen Scott's identification, there was no reason to think otherwise. The prescriptions were now included in Scott's medical records as part of his medical history. During one of the many phone conversations he had with insurance representatives, Scott wondered aloud how Nick had come by those prescriptions in the first place. Had a real doctor prescribed them? And if so, had the doctor known Nick's real identity?

"The customer rep said that, worst-case scenario, Nick had gone into a doctor's office as me and had been treated and prescribed as me. Or he could have falsified a prescription. It seemed like the further I got into it, the more convoluted it got. But I was still willing to give him the benefit of the doubt, right up until I got a call from the pharmacy asking for Davy, my three-year-old son."

Con men and women vary in approach, motivation, and experience. Some are professional, long-time scam artists. Others have fallen into the con game as a result of circumstance and are not as practiced. They may have taken up a life of crime to support a drug habit. They may project an image of wealth and refinement. They may be aggressive or smooth talking or both. A conner may look like the girl next door or the scary hitchhiker from a horror movie. There is no way to know just by looking.

They may also look very familiar. Don't make the mistake of thinking that because you know someone or because you have something in common with someone, that he or she is trustworthy. There are dishonest folks among our neighbors, acquaintances, and even family. Why would someone you know try to scam you? It's less work. They already have your trust, or think they do. They have easy access. Your guard is down. You're more likely to say yes to whatever they ask, especially if they claim to be in need or in trouble. If it's a relative, he or she may use guilt to manipulate your emotions. People who share something in common with you—a member of the same club or congregation, a classmate—can also trade on that association to gain your trust. The perpetrator may turn out to be someone you have known for years, such as a close friend, a relative, a confidante. These relationships can make it harder for victims to differentiate between a crime and a simple mistake or bad judgment on the part of the perpetrator.

The pharmacist who called Scott was filling a prescription for Davy and had found a discrepancy. The prescription was for a sleeping pill, but it conflicted with another medication he had already been prescribed. From the way the pharmacist was talking, it was clear he believed Davy was an adult. Scott was horrified.

"Davy's not on any prescriptions. He's a toddler. I couldn't believe it. I thought, it can't be. Nick wouldn't do that to me, to my family. But he had. Now he was using my baby's name to get drugs. I was furious. My wife went ballistic. This time I knew I had to go straight to the police. I couldn't go back to Nick because obviously he was a liar and a thief and he had no intention of stopping. What shocked me the most was that he was not at all the person I thought he was. It was chilling."

When Scott finally went to the authorities, they found that Nick had been poaching from dozens of people, not only employees, but relatives as well. With access to all his employees' personnel files, he was able to obtain Social Security and insurance information that allowed him to impersonate them. Most of the pills were for personal consumption, but Nick also occasionally sold prescription painkillers.

"I was surprised at how easy it was for him to co-opt someone else's identity," says Scott. "These systems define us; it's not who we are as people. Apparently as long as you have the right numbers and cards to plug into the system, no one is going to question you."

Scott left his job, and the company eventually folded, but it took him months to rectify the mistakes in his and Davy's medical records.

MANY FACES OF FRAUD

Scam, sham, con, grift, bunco, flimflam, swindle, fiddle, hustle. The English language has no shortage of words to describe fraud, many of which make it sound playful, almost like a child's card game. But make no mistake. Fraud is a serious crime and it is rampant.

The Federal Trade Commission (FTC) reports that more than 30 million Americans a year fall victim to fraud, with nearly 50 million reported incidents of consumer fraud, including fake foreign lotteries, prize promotions, work-at-home programs, and pyramid schemes. No one thinks it can happen to them, but Americans are 40 times more likely to be defrauded than to have their cars stolen or their homes burgled. Con artists ruin people financially and emotionally, leaving in their wake a trail of destruction, broken hearts, and deflated dreams.

The declining housing market, financial collapse of 2008, and subsequent recession highlighted an epidemic of financial scams that both precipitated and made use of deteriorating economic conditions. In response, President Barack Obama established the Financial Fraud Enforcement Task Force, a broad coalition of law enforcement, investigatory, and regulatory government agencies and departments charged with investigating and prosecuting significant financial crimes, including mortgage and tax fraud, credit card theft, and Ponzi schemes. The FTC created "Operation Short Change" to target criminals taking advantage of the economic crisis to fleece people through employment scams, get rich quick schemes, and fraudulent benefits or debt reduction services.

The epidemic shows no signs of abating. An Associated Press analysis of scams across the country found that 150 Ponzi schemes collapsed in 2009, as compared with approximately 40 the year before. These failed schemes, based on fraudulent investments, represent a loss of $16.5 billion to investors. This includes only Ponzi schemes that were detected and prosecuted. Untold numbers continue under the radar of law enforcement. Identity theft, one of the most highly publicized forms of fraud, has been steadily increasing year over year. An annual identity theft survey conducted by Javelin Strategy and Research reveals that in 2009, 11 million Americans were victims of identity theft, to the tune of $54 billion. Fraud involving checking accounts is also on the rise. The American Bankers Association reported increases in nearly every area of fraud covered in its annual survey, including more than 760,000 cases of check fraud and debit card fraud totaling $788 million.

Advances in technology have made it easier for scams to flourish, reaching millions of potential victims at once through avenues such as e-mail, texting, short message service (SMS), instant messaging (IM), robocalls, and social networking. The Internet Crime Complaint Center (IC3), a partnership between the Federal Bureau of Investigation, the National White Collar Crime Center, and the Bureau of Justice Assistance, solicits complaints in the area of cybercrime and, when appropriate, refers them to the relevant law enforcement or regulatory agencies. In its most recent annual Internet Crime Report, IC3 noted that complaint submissions had increased by more than 22 percent, with losses reported at nearly $560 million.

These statistics involve only reported instances of fraud. There is no way of knowing exactly how many cons are attempted in any given time period. Many scam victims are hesitant to report the crimes because they are embarrassed at having been duped. As one victim put it, she felt like the "dummy of the year" after falling for a swindle. Many people don't want to admit having been taken in by a con. In cases where the victim is related to or acquainted with the perpetrator, there may be an increased reluctance to report the person to the police. In such instances, the swindlers may also attempt to negotiate with their victims in order to avoid police attention. People scammed by family members may not even consider the act a crime. Others blame themselves and view the loss as their own fault.

Some victims feel remorse because the money stolen was not theirs. One woman borrowed money from her ill mother and was devastated when she lost it to a con man posing as a suitor. A man who tapped into his daughter's college savings fund to invest in a "sure thing" without his family's knowledge attempted to keep the loss a secret. In such cases, feelings of anger are compounded by deep guilt. All these factors keep the number of reported fraud cases to only a fraction of the actual amount.

Even though the crime is underreported, existing figures are alarming enough to cause concern. Unfortunately, scams are still often viewed as peripheral crimes. Becoming a victim of fraud doesn't seem as scary as being mugged. If someone tried to mug you every time you went to the store, you would probably change your behavior or vary your routine. Yet people are bombarded by scam solicitations on a near daily basis and do nothing. In an ideal world, you would never encounter a con artist, but the likelihood is that you already have, on more occasions than you can count. Anyone with an e-mail address has read a phishing message. Anyone with a phone can receive a phony alert call. The simple act of walking on the street can attract strangers peddling scams.

Art dealer and gallery owner Lawrence Salander was a prominent figure in the New York art world for 30 years. Among his clients were tennis superstar John McEnroe, the estate of artist Robert De Niro Sr., and the heirs of American artists Stuart Davis and Ralston Crawford. A 2008 profile in *New York* magazine describes him as "a prophet and a gambler" whose "gravitational pull" drew in both creators and collectors of fine art. The very next year, Salander was in a Manhattan courtroom facing 100 criminal charges, including forgery, fraud, and grand larceny. Salander was accused of selling artwork belonging to his clients without their consent or knowledge, and pocketing the proceeds. As the case against him unfolded, it became clear that for Salander, art was a form of currency he used to stave off creditors, as collateral to underwrite additional debt, and to defraud investors. He eventually pled guilty, expressed remorse, and received a prison sentence of 6 to 18 years. His case drew attention because of the celebrity of those involved and also because of the scale of the fraud, estimated at $120 million.

Earl Davis, son of painter Stuart Davis, was a close friend turned victim of Salander's. The theft of 90 of his father's paintings was a deeply traumatic experience for Davis. As was widely reported, he said, "Had I been robbed at gunpoint or by a thief in the night, it would have been preferable to the ruthlessly drawn out torture that he inflicted upon me."

Salander's story contains all the elements of a Hollywood movie—money, betrayal, fame—but in essence it is no different from any other scam ever perpetrated. The prosecution's characterization of Salander as a "pathological, self-absorbed con man" could apply to anyone who's conned an innocent person. High-profile cases like Salander's and that of disgraced financier Bernie Madoff generate publicity because of the immense sums and high-society figures involved, but they only serve to highlight a crime that is pervasive and destructive and can strike anyone at any time.

EASY OPENING

A mother receives a phone call saying her soldier son has been injured in Iraq. A college student finds the perfect part-time job. A prospective tenant responds to a couple's online classified ad. A man exchanges instant messages with an old friend in trouble. A company in Texas creates a miracle weight-loss powder. An office worker returning from lunch finds a lost wallet.

These seemingly innocuous events are all the opening acts to scams carried out on ordinary people far from the limelight. The circumstances and storylines vary greatly, but in each case, the intended consequence was the same—to swindle someone. In each case, there were no weapons involved, no physical intimidation, and no dark alleys. But the threat of harm, of financial ruin, and emotional devastation, was just as menacing. For those who are victimized by scams, the consequences can be even more harmful than a physical confrontation. The sentiments expressed by victim Earl Davis accurately depict the emotional and psychological violence inflicted by cons.

Why, then, are people slow or reluctant to recognize scams as a serious threat?

For one thing, a con artist does not wear a stocking over his or her face and carry a gun. It's not so easy to see him or her coming. There's usually no sense of immediate danger or a threat to physical safety. Detection and avoidance are made more difficult by the fact that con artists target their victims in a myriad of ways. Unlike the mugger, whose strategy will generally involve approaching a victim, demanding money, perhaps brandishing a weapon, the scammer will employ stealth tactics, duplicity, disguise, whatever it takes to lower your defenses. The con may take the form of a business proposal, a romantic relationship, or an urgent appeal. It may come camouflaged as good news or the very worst news. And unlike a physical attack, victims may not even realize a crime has been committed until long after the swindle has taken place.

Scammers do not fit any single demographic profile. Potential perpetrators include those we look to for advice or assistance. Doctors, lawyers, clergy members, financial advisers, brokers, bankers, and other professional individuals project an air of authority. We rely on them for their expertise, and in most instances, they are reliable and helpful. This does not mean, however, that we should accept everything they propose or say without questioning. They are in possession of sensitive medical, financial, and other personal information that could allow them to take advantage of their clients. Then again, the scammer could be a random stranger who comes up to you on the street or calls you on the phone. It can be someone halfway around the world. With the technology available today, you may never even see or hear the person who is trying to swindle you.

There is a myth that scams, particularly those involving financial institutions, are somehow "victimless" crimes if the individuals are not held liable for the monetary losses or if they receive restitution from the criminals. No one who has actually been a victim of a scam could find this argument plausible. Whenever someone you know or think you know betrays your trust or a complete stranger invades your life for personal gain, there is an emotional cost. In addition, even when the financial institution assumes liability, the victim is still left to sort out the mess and put matters right.

Complicating the issue is the fact that degrees of deception exist everywhere in our daily lives. The supermarket chain that exhorts us to "spend more to save more" or the diet shake that promises a smaller waistline use deceptive practices to sell us a product or service. Truth in advertising is generally accepted to be an oxymoron. With the advent of tools such as CGI, auto-tuning, and Photoshop, technology has facilitated a certain level of deception. On some occasions, we find it desirable. We like to hear that we are attractive or clever or good at what we do, even if we have a sneaking suspicion that we're not. We withhold or temper the truth when we think it might hurt those we love. We criticize totalitarian states for creating their own versions of the truth, but democratic governments also rely on propaganda to gain public support for their initiatives. Although we claim to value the truth above all things, we have concocted the term "white lie" to distinguish a harmless or unimportant lie from a full-blown deceit.

The proliferation of deceit in the public arena has led to deep cynicism toward elected officials and public figures. In 1994, the chief executives of seven major U.S. tobacco companies took the stand at a congressional hearing chaired by Rep. Henry Waxman (D-Calif.). In his opening remarks, Waxman seemed to foreshadow coming events by saying, "It is sometimes easier to invent fiction than to face the truth." All seven executives went on to testify under oath that they did not believe nicotine was addictive. Their denial of something widely accepted as fact strained belief and was considered a turning point in the fight against Big Tobacco. It was an extreme example of the kind of misrepresentation that permeates public life.

In short, we are used to people lying to us. We have come to expect it. The boundary between truth and falsehood has been blurred, and occasionally the nature of truth itself becomes debatable. If we didn't have YouTube to remind us, it might be difficult to believe that a sitting president, Bill Clinton, once uttered the infamous words, "It depends upon what the meaning of the word 'is' is."

All around us there are shades of gray. The truth can be manipulated. This is an environment in which scams flourish. Con artists are liars, but if lying is not always perceived as negative, how do we know when we should beware? How can we tell a malevolent lie from a slick marketing tactic? When is someone truly in peril and when is the person crying wolf? How do we separate an evangelist's promise of life everlasting from a grifter's guarantee of earthly abundance, especially if they are both asking us for money? How do we separate what *sounds* good from what is *true*? Being able to make these distinctions is an important part of sifting out the dangerous from the merely distracting.

Our lack of wariness regarding fraudsters is also due in part to how they are often portrayed in popular culture, as charming, harmless rogues or even heroes. Think Robert Redford and Paul Newman in *The Sting*, Ryan O'Neal in *Paper Moon*, or Steve Martin, Michael Caine, and Glenne Headly in *Dirty Rotten Scoundrels*. And who wouldn't be won over by the rakish crew George Clooney leads in *Ocean's Eleven, Twelve*, and *Thirteen*? These sanitized versions of con artists inhabit a world in which their actions are not so much evil as mischievous. Those swindlers who are acknowledged as criminals are usually redeemed, as with the dashing rascal Sawyer in the television series *Lost*. The implication is that these people are to be admired more than they are to be feared. Their victims are inconsequential or deserving of what they get. These are not people who are out to get you or me. They are certainly not threatening or sociopathic. This diverges greatly from reality, in which scam artists are self-centered, dangerous, and amoral, with no regard for their victims.

PLAYING THE GAME

Gabrielle is a young single mother who became ensnared in a scam. A storefront establishment billing itself as a tax preparation company promised her an expedited tax refund for a fee. She paid the money and never received her refund. When she followed up with the company, the tax preparer said additional payment was required. When Gabrielle refused, the woman threatened to report her to the IRS for nonpayment of taxes. Although Gabrielle was innocent, she was also unfamiliar with tax law and the thought of being reported terrified her, so she complied. More time went by and she still had not received her refund. In need of the money, she returned to the office and was told that she was not owed a refund after all. When Gabrielle threatened to complain to the police, the tax preparer pointed to a piece of paper on her desk and said, "I have your name, your Social, your address. I can make trouble for you." Concerned for her safety and that of her daughter, Gabrielle never went to the police.

This is not the kind of intimidating scenario people generally conjure up when thinking about scams in the real world. We have a vague awareness that they exist, but we think they are easily avoided and less harmful than annoying. Scams are anecdotes told as a form of entertainment.

This complacency puts us in a vulnerable position. There are certain precautions we take as a matter of routine. We know that seat restraints can save lives. So when we get in our cars, we automatically reach for the seat belt. We wear sunscreen. We avoid dark alleys. We make sure our doors are locked before we go to sleep. We tell our kids not to talk to strangers. None of these things are guaranteed to save us, but they significantly reduce our risk. We think we do everything we can to safeguard ourselves and our families from harm. But we're human. We leave our bags unattended. We open the door to salespeople. We stop to help strangers. We put our checks in the mailbox. We answer the phone. We go online. Each of these actions opens us up to the possibility of being scammed. And as the numbers prove, it works.

So what can we do about it?

Scams differ from other crimes in that they usually require a degree of consent on the part of the victim in order to succeed. The con relies on a victim agreeing to hand over money, share personal information, or otherwise contribute to his or her own fleecing. Consequently, many people feel they are partially to blame for their own misfortune. This is the bad news. The good news is that it also means, if spotted in time, the vast majority of scams are *avoidable*.

Intelligent people can act foolishly at any time. Successful scams do not require victims to be especially gullible. All they need to be fruitful is momentary believability. Even the most judicious, cautious people can display temporary lapses in judgment. In order to protect ourselves, we must learn how to train our brains to assess and reject advances, encounters, approaches, and communications that do not meet sufficient standards of credibility.

The purpose of this book is to help you recognize the signs of a scam. The key to avoiding scams and the crooks who perpetrate them is to develop a "safety first" mindset.

Erring on the side of caution goes a long way. Most people, if asked, would say that they could spot a scam if they saw one. However, if scams were that easy to pick out, tens of millions of people a year would not be victimized. Here is a simple experiment. The next time you are in a gathering of people, ask if any of them or anyone they know has been the victim of a scam. The probability is that at least one story will emerge, and the victim will not be someone who appears especially exploitable. The difference between those who fall for a scam and those who don't has nothing to do with levels of education, intelligence, or income. It has everything to do with receptivity and reaction.

Many people think it could never happen to them. They hear stories of scams and their response is, "I would never fall for that." This false sense of security is hazardous because it causes us to take risks in the belief that we are somehow untouchable or that the chances of getting hurt are slim.

Retiree Ivan has been investing since his early 20s. As a seasoned investor, he prides himself on always doing his homework before handing over a check. When one of his favorite local radio hosts began touting an investment fund, it peaked his interest and he looked into it. Going online, he found nothing negative, no evidence of shady dealings or history of disgruntled investors. The radio host's position as an established media figure also added to Ivan's confidence. He handed over nearly all of his savings, more than $310,000. Unfortunately for Ivan, he became a disgruntled investor when his savings vanished. The fund was a Ponzi scheme based on nonexistent shares in a phony company. Ivan's life savings had gone to pay for the host's lavish home, boat, and other luxury items. Although Ivan felt he had done his research, in this case, the signs that something was amiss were not to be found on the Web. Instead, the warning signs were evident in inflated promises made by the radio host, which included guaranteed returns of 15 percent or more.

SELF-DEFENSE

Self-defense against scams begins with a holistic approach. There is a lot you can do to reduce your chances of being conned. The first is to reduce risky behavior on all fronts. Consistency is essential because scammers can infiltrate from a number of different directions. Having an expensive alarm system in your home is not going to help you if the back door is left wide open. Similarly, choosing a complex computer password is pointless if you have to write it on your desk calendar to remember it. Shredding your mail is helpful, but leaving your checkbook in the car is not. You may think you live in a safe neighborhood, but it only takes one incident to become a victim.

Laurie is a police officer who specializes in community education. Whenever she sees purses or bags left unattended in shopping carts, she makes a point of leaving her card on top of the bag with a note telling the owners to be more careful. A gesture as small as leaving your possessions unattended to get a cup of coffee may not seem precarious, but if you return to find something stolen, the inconvenience to you will be far greater than it would have been if you'd taken the things with you.

A study sponsored by the Dell computer company found that 12,000 laptops a week are lost, go missing, or are stolen at airports nationwide. That's 624,000 laptops a year. Astonishingly, of the laptops that are located and returned to the airport lost and found, two-thirds are *never* reclaimed by their owners. On an individual level, a laptop in the wrong hands is as good as a key to your door or to your bank account. And if the computers are used for work, companies, organizations, and government agencies are at risk for data breaches that could affect millions, expose sensitive national security information, or put lives in danger. The Department of Defense recently revealed that the most serious data breach the Pentagon ever experienced was caused by the insertion of a flash drive into a military laptop in the Middle East. This simple act by a foreign intelligence agency allowed a malicious code to spread through military computer networks for the purposes of transferring classified material back to the unnamed foreign power.

You probably don't have a laptop that can access U.S. Central Command, but that doesn't make you any less attractive to the run-of-the-mill con artist. Just as the malicious code infiltrated U.S. military computer systems, a swindler is like a parasite looking for a way into your life. Like the code, the swindler is looking for something—information, money, or both. The swindler needs the host in order to survive and thrive. In most cases, it doesn't matter how rich, powerful, attractive, or smart the host is. All that matters is that there is a relatively easy way in, and that the host has something the parasite wants. In some cases, scammers prefer to keep a low profile so their victims don't even know they're being preyed upon. Other cases require the hosts' active participation. Either way, given a choice, crooks will choose the path of least resistance.

To avoid these parasites altogether, make life more difficult for them. There are practical, immediate steps you can take to help protect yourself. Most of these are straightforward. Keeping your possessions close at hand at all times shouldn't be too difficult. Monitoring your credit reports requires some initiative, but not much. Verifying identities and sources may take a few phone calls but is easily done. These actions are simple but crucial. What may prove more challenging are the forms of self-defense that involve reading human behavior and developing a sixth sense about scams. This comes into play when interacting directly with a con artist.

We are not trained in recognizing deceitful behavior even though it exists all around us. Even when we know that we are being lied to, it's not always easy to tell how. More than one game show has traded on this concept, presenting contestants with a series of falsehoods or imposters and asking them to pick out the individual telling the truth. Some of us are more predisposed than others to be suspicious, but those who practice deceit as a profession are very good at what they do. They will anticipate skepticism and prepare for it by having explanations and excuses for every question or objection. Con artists sometimes delude themselves into thinking that there is some truth to what they are saying, making their pitches that much more convincing.

We have to take responsibility for our own safety. To really make a difference, we need to create a filter through which we pass all communications we receive. Just as we install virus software on our computers, we need to have within us a built-in scam scan that becomes instinctive and runs continually in the background. Once you figure out what to look for, defending yourself against scams should be second nature, just as instinctive as putting on a seat belt.

The first step to combating fraud is to take it seriously, to realize how pernicious and widespread cons are. The next step is to understand it. Chapters 2 and 3 will explore in more detail the anatomy of a con and why cons are successful. Knowing the elements of a con will help you with detection and will enable you to recognize vulnerabilities in everyday life so you can strengthen these areas of weakness. For example, you will understand why you should never put certain bumper stickers on your car. Or hold a stranger's money.

The remainder of the book divides scams into seven categories, with each category representing a point of entry by which a conner can gain access to you and your assets. The last chapter is dedicated to recovering from identity theft. Each chapter on scams ends with a list of ways to help avoid that particular genre of scam. Just as there are characteristics common to all scams, there are protective measures that can be applied uniformly to defend against them. Going behind the scenes of real-world cons allows us to examine the logistics and psychology of scams as they are enacted.

Scams are in most cases crimes of persuasion and storytelling, and the stories presented here are of ordinary people from all walks of life thrown into unexpected and disorienting circumstances. The scams portrayed are all based on real cons currently in use. However, specific details, circumstances, characters, and names have been altered. The experiences related here provide a variety of perspectives and illustrate how scams work in everyday life.

Scams are nothing new. They have been around in one form or another for as long as humans have. The only difference between the ancient con and the modern con is that technology has made it faster, easier, and more lucrative to scam even larger numbers of people. With the click of a mouse, identities can be stolen, bank accounts drained, credit cards charged. This is not to say that the low-tech scam no longer exists; on the contrary, it is alive and well. Being a technophobe will not protect you. What will help protect you are a few practical safeguards and a good working knowledge of what scams look and sound like. There are certain telltale signs of fraud, some of which are quite subtle. The goal is to help you understand and recognize deception, and in the same way that you would avoid other potentially dangerous situations, take a detour.

(2)

KNOW THE ENEMY

Elements of a Con

Rosie returned from her 25th high school reunion flushed with nostalgia and excited at having reestablished contact with so many old friends. The reunion organizer set up a page on a social networking site where alumni could share photos, post messages, and link up with one another. Rosie posted her photos immediately and exchanged messages with classmates who had been at the reunion. Several of those who had not attended logged on to see what they had missed. One day, Rosie received a message through the site. The subject line read, "Remember me?"

Scams begin one of two ways. The swindler can contact the target directly or set the bait and wait for the target to make the first move. In either case, there must be sufficient plausibility and good faith for the target to proceed.

"He said his name was Julian, and he'd been a year behind me in high school. I couldn't place him, so I looked in my senior yearbook and there he was in the junior section. The face looked familiar, and I saw that we had both been in the band, but we hadn't known each other very well. Still, we did have a shared connection, so I wrote back and we started an e-mail correspondence."

MEET AND GREET

Almost all cons have several elements in common. The first is the meet and greet portion, where the con artist establishes his or her identity, whether real or fraudulent. Scammers also offer justification for their presence and behavior, just as an actor searches for the key to a character by asking, "What's my motivation?"

What constitutes identity depends on the scam. In Rosie's case, identity consisted of a whole persona and a shared history. In other scams, where the encounter is briefer, it may be something as simple as a name and occupation. "I'm Sam and I'm calling from the Internal Revenue Service." Or it may be established in writing, through official-looking letterhead and forms. It's amazing what the addition of a seal or bar code will do to make a piece of paper look legitimate. Whatever form this step takes, it serves two purposes: to put the intended victim at ease and to lend credibility for what is to come. If the target accepts the perpetrator's identity, expertise, or credentials as legitimate, the scam can continue on to the next phase.

THE SETUP

Over a period of weeks, Rosie and Julian exchanged dozens of messages. Although Rosie had not known Julian well, the fact that they had gone to high school together gave her an instant level of comfort and familiarity with him. "There was certainly a feeling of kinship there," she admits. "We had walked the same hallways, endured the same teachers. We'd even played music together. I could tell from his messages that he was smart and had a good sense of humor."

At first, the communications mostly involved exchanging memories of high school, but they quickly moved into writing about everyday experiences and sharing tidbits of their personal lives. They began calling and texting one another. Rosie lived in North Carolina; Julian said he lived in New York. She was single and had never married. He was divorced with a teenage daughter living in California. He told Rosie he was on bad terms with his ex-wife and didn't see his daughter as much as he'd like. She sympathized.

"We were just two ordinary people exchanging life stories, but I really started to look forward to getting his calls and e-mails. When I heard my phone ping to tell me a text had arrived, I always hoped it would be him. It did feel romantic. We became close very quickly. He was easy to talk to, and we had a lot in common. We discussed visiting one another, but I'm a teacher, so it's tough for me to get away during the school year. And he had his own business, so he was also tied to that. But we were thinking winter break would be a good opportunity for me to get up to New York."

After the pair had been corresponding for three months, Rosie called Julian one day to find him sounding downcast. At first he denied anything was wrong, but after a while, he shared the source of his distress. Julian had kept one secret from Rosie. He suffered from a chronic illness.

"I didn't know anything about hepatitis. I thought it was something that people in Third World countries get, like malaria. He felt so bad that he hadn't told me, especially since we'd shared so much of ourselves and this was something major in his life. My mother died of cancer when I was in high school, so I know something about serious illness. I know how grueling and painful it can be, both emotionally and physically. My heart went out to him. But this wasn't cancer. He had lived with it for years and said his symptoms were fairly mild."

His spirits lifted, Julian asked Rosie if she would still come visit over the holidays, as they had planned. She readily agreed. A month later, she was on a plane to New York. Julian met her at the airport with a spray of orchids, her favorite flower. Rosie was charmed instantly. On the cab ride from the airport, Rosie, who was unfamiliar with New York City, asked him where he lived in relation to the city's famous landmarks.

"He didn't really answer the question. Instead, he said we wouldn't be staying in his apartment after all. He said his building had been infested with bedbugs and was being fumigated, so he was temporarily staying in one of those extended stay hotels. That's where we were headed."

Rosie was surprised. She and Julian usually shared every piece of news in their lives, but this was the first she'd heard of the bedbug problem. "I didn't want to pursue it. I thought he was probably just embarrassed and irritated by the inconvenience of being put out of his apartment, especially when I was coming."

That exchange was the only odd note in what turned out to be a fairytale trip for Rosie. Julian was every bit as chivalrous, witty, and thoughtful as she had expected. The duo visited museums, shopped, ate, took in a Broadway show, went to the top of the Empire State Building and admired the Christmas scene at Rockefeller Center. Although Julian claimed to feel fine, Rosie noticed he tired easily and needed an afternoon nap to make it through the day. His appetite also seemed to ebb and flow.

On the last night of Rosie's stay, they went out for a cozy dinner at an Indian restaurant in the neighborhood. As she and Julian reviewed some of the highlights of the week, Rosie was filled with a feeling of deep contentment. Even in hindsight, with all that happened, the trip remains a happy memory for her. "It was fabulous. You can't take that away from me."

THE ASK

With Rosie back in North Carolina, she and Julian picked up where they had left off with their routine of calling, texting, and e-mailing several times a day. Then one day, there was no communication from Julian. Rosie, who was used to starting her day with an e-mail from him, saw nothing in her inbox. She went into work and became engrossed in the day's activities. It wasn't until lunchtime that she began to worry. There had been no call, not even a brief text message. She tried calling him and got his voicemail every time.

It wasn't until late in the evening that he finally called. "His voice sounded all funny, like maybe he'd been crying. I asked him what had happened. He said that the hepatitis had escalated to liver disease. The doctor told him he needed a liver transplant. So then I started crying. It was a mess. I had a lot of questions. Could he get a liver? Was there a waiting list? How long would it take? How did it work? But he didn't want to talk about it. He said he'd been thinking about it all day, trying to take it in. He was understandably depressed. So I just let it go and tried to comfort him as best I could."

The next day, Rosie called back to check on Julian. He was calmer, almost resigned to his fate. But when Rosie heard him talking about plans to get his affairs in order, she became alarmed. "I asked him why he was talking like that. Had the doctors said it was hopeless? Apparently not. A liver transplant would save him, but he had decided against it. I couldn't believe it. I asked him why, and he changed the subject."

Later, as she was mulling over the conversation, Rosie remembered something Julian had said in one of their earlier exchanges about his business not doing too well. His commercial construction company had been badly hit by the recession. Rosie recalled him expressing remorse over being forced to let employees go when the work dwindled.

The next time they spoke, Rosie confronted Julian about his reasons for not pursuing a transplant. At first he was evasive, but he eventually admitted that in an effort to save costs, he had let his health insurance policy lapse and was paying out of pocket for all the doctors' visits.

"He had alimony and child support payments, and he was adamant that he wasn't going to be a deadbeat dad. He would rather sacrifice his own well-being than hurt his daughter. And a transplant isn't cheap. The figure he quoted was somewhere in the neighborhood of $300,000. Bottom line, he couldn't afford to do it and he was going to let the disease take its course. It made no sense to me, and I got angry. So that conversation did not end well."

In the setup stage, the con artist presents a backstory that will serve as the foundation of the scam. The more sophisticated the scam, the more extensive the setup will be. In a period of less than six months, Julian had entered Rosie's life, developed an intense friendship with her, and was now seemingly in danger of dying.

Imagine sitting across a table from someone. Your wallet is out in front of you. If your companion wants your money, there are two ways to get it. One way is to grab the wallet. The other is for you to hand it over. But since you are unlikely to relinquish your wallet without good reason, you'll need to be persuaded. A convincing setup and an artful swindler will have you handing over your wallet obligingly. You may even think it was your own idea.

After their argument, Rosie received a bouquet of flowers from Julian. He apologized for burdening her with all the emotional baggage and negativity associated with his illness. He said she would have been better off if he had never written to her, and if she wished, he would cease all contact. Rosie would have none of it. She couldn't stop thinking about

Julian's predicament. She felt invested in their relationship, undefined and brief as it was, and she cared about him.

"I felt as though we had just started out on this journey and didn't know where it would lead. Someone had put up a big stop sign to prevent us from going any further, but why did we have to accept it? I wasn't willing to do that. And I hoped he wasn't either."

Late one night, he texted her, asking if she was awake. She was, and so they began another of their marathon phone exchanges. "He was all excited. He'd seen some story on TV about this thing called medical tourism, where he could go to Asia and get his transplant done for a fraction of the cost. At first I thought he was kidding. It sounded completely insane to me."

But Julian had done some independent research and found that he could travel to Thailand and have the procedure done for around $60,000, including airfare. He admitted the price was still out of reach, but at least it offered him some hope. Despite her skepticism, Rosie was glad to hear him sounding enthusiastic and upbeat, so she played along as the two of them brainstormed ways to raise the money. Selling what was left of his business was one option, but it was time-consuming and not guaranteed to happen. His apartment was a rental and there were no other assets to speak of. Julian joked that his best hope might be to win the lottery.

"He said, 'If only I was a trust fund baby.' I said there had to be a way. He said, 'Yeah, maybe we could have a bake sale at your school.' I chuckled, but it got me thinking that maybe there was something I could do. I own a house. I have savings. I am not a trust fund baby, but my mother was, and when she died, I inherited a healthy chunk of that. That's how I was able to become a homeowner at a young age on a single teacher's salary."

If the ultimate goal of every con is to enrich the swindler, there will come a point when the subject must be broached. In the "ask" segment of a con, the target is asked to provide money or personal information that will be used to acquire his or her money. The ask can be an outright request or demand for funds or something more subtle and nuanced. Julian did not ask Rosie directly for money, but he steered her to the conclusion that she could and should help finance his transplant. When the whole episode was over, it was this phase more than any other that Rosie revisited.

"At first I was sure it was all my idea, but the more I thought about it, the more things came back to me. Little comments he would make about money, casual questions about my retirement, my mortgage, the money my mother had left me. It was always in the context of sharing personal stories, but in hindsight, I think he was working me all the time. Isn't that one of the top 10 tips for making a successful sale, to manipulate the customer into thinking it was all their idea? I even wonder if he knew in advance that my mother had died and left me that money. I wouldn't be surprised. And boy did he do a good job of appearing totally taken aback when I suggested that I loan him the money. As if it never would have occurred to him in a million years."

CARROT OR STICK

The benefits of action for Rosie were clear. If she was able to help Julian fund his treatment and it was successful, as she believed it would be, there was the potential of a happy future together. She had always wanted to get married and had almost given up hope that she would ever meet someone worth marrying. Julian had been unlucky in love, but now he too had a second chance. His appearance in her life had been completely unexpected, in a wonderful and exhilarating way. A transplant was always a gamble, especially under these conditions, yet she felt it was not only worthwhile but absolutely necessary.

When Rosie brought up the subject of funding his trip herself, a shocked Julian at first refused. When he eventually accepted the offer, he insisted it was a loan to be repaid with interest. She agreed. In return, she asked to see a detailed plan for the trip and treatment. Julian sent her a packet of information that included a bio of the doctor who would be performing the transplant, a fact sheet on the hospital, an itinerary, and a signed letter from Julian's American doctor lending his support for the plan. He also sent her a YouTube clip of an American man who had successfully undergone a similar procedure overseas.

"He kept telling me the doctor had gone to Harvard Medical School. That was the big selling point for him. He was so excited, so happy, so grateful. His enthusiasm was infectious. I also thought it was fitting in

some way that this money my mother had left me be used to save someone's life. What could be more noble?"

If the establishment of a swindler's identity provides his or her motivation, the presentation of a carrot or stick serves as the victim's motivation. At the heart of every classic con looms the threat of grave consequences or the promise of a large reward. Something must compel the
victim to act, whether it is fear, hope, greed, love, or some other strong
emotion. Rosie's situation carried both a threat and a promise. If she did
nothing, her relationship was likely over before it had even really begun.
If she took the initiative, the rewards could be limitless—true love, happiness, matrimony, a family.

ACT NOW

Julian's doctors were in agreement that his time frame was limited. His
liver was failing and soon he would be too ill to travel. He told Rosie he
needed $5,000 immediately for a series of tests to be run in New York,
the results of which would be shared with the doctor in Thailand. She
sent him the money.

Urgency is a common characteristic of scams. Immediate action is
required in order to avoid the bad or receive the good. Swindlers want
to get their hands on the money as soon as possible. They also want to
avoid being discovered. The longer the con goes on, the more chance
there is that the target will get cold feet or become suspicious and go to
the police. In cases where there is some financial reward at stake, presenting the situation as urgent gives the victim the impression that he
or she is privy to something special. For instance, someone peddling a
phony investment scam might say, "I can get you in on the ground floor,
but you have to do it today, before other people get wind of it. We're
approaching a small number of handpicked investors, and you're one of
them. Act now, or live forever with the regret."

Rosie asked Julian when he would be leaving. He said that as soon
as he had the money, he could book his flight. According to him, the
transplant fees had to be paid up front in cash. He instructed her to wire
him the money; he would then take care of sending it on to the hospital.
When she went into the bank to arrange the wire transfer, the account

manager, whom she knew well, inquired why she was withdrawing such a large sum of money.

"I said he wouldn't believe me if I told him. I said it was for a good deed and left it at that. And it was a good deed. Being able to help Julian made me feel good. It brought us closer together. If I couldn't give him my own liver, this was the next best thing. Love is a risk, and I was putting all my chips on the table, literally. I wanted to go with him, but he said he didn't want to expose me to the whole hospital scene. He said we'd go back to Thailand together when he was healthy again and we'd be proper tourists."

HIGH-PRESSURE TACTICS

The money had been sent and Julian's trip was set. He was due to leave on a Monday morning. On Friday afternoon, Rosie was grading papers in her classroom when she received an emergency phone call. It was a woman's voice. She said she was Julian's neighbor. He had been taken from the building by ambulance earlier in the day, and as he passed her in the hall, he had hurriedly asked her to call Rosie and tell her what had happened.

"I asked what hospital he had been taken to. She didn't know. So I called his cell phone. Of course it went straight to voicemail. There wasn't much else I could do for the moment, but I was terrified. Three or four hours later, when I was at home, I got a text from him, just one brief line saying he was okay and he'd call me the next day. I didn't sleep at all that night."

When Julian called the next day, he said he'd been kept overnight in the hospital for observation after feeling dizzy and nauseous in his apartment. Rosie asked if he'd still be able to travel to Thailand on Monday. She was thinking of the length of the flight and the toll of the travel on Julian's weakened system. He dismissed her concern.

"He said that when he got back, if all went well with the transplant, he was going to move down to North Carolina to be with me. He said he'd already looked into the property market in my area and he believed his business could thrive there. I was thrilled."

Anyone who has been swayed by a particularly talented salesperson is one step away from succumbing to the powers of persuasion exercised by successful con artists. A practiced scammer is persuasive and insistent. Sometimes the insistence is couched in charm; other times, it carries an implicit or explicit threat. Once the carrot or stick is dangled, the high-pressure tactics are used to keep the victim moving in the right direction. Julian's relapse, hospital stay, and talk of their post-surgery relationship served to heighten all of Rosie's feelings. She experienced increased anxiety at the possibility of losing him. She felt validation that she'd made the right decision in helping him. She was excited about and focused on their future together.

"I thought, if we can make it through this, my life is going to be completely different. It's going to be better. Much better. I was very hopeful."

KEEP IT TO YOURSELF

With so many momentous events taking place in her life, Rosie was eager to share everything with her close friends and family, but from the outset, Julian had sworn her to secrecy. Before he'd ever mentioned being sick, he asked her to keep their communications and relationship under wraps. His reasons varied. He said he was a private person. He didn't want people gossiping about him. He didn't want it to get around the network of alumni from their high school. He also mentioned that his ex-wife was stalking him online and looking to dig up dirt to use against him. For all these reasons, he preferred to keep a low profile.

"Then when he began talking about this transplant in Thailand, he said we really had to keep it all hush-hush. I wasn't too clear on the details, but it had to do with laws regarding transplants and donors both in the U.S. and over there. He implied that it was kind of a gray area legally. I never asked about the donor. To be honest, I didn't want to know who the donor was, if it was a living person or someone deceased. I assumed it was a living donor, otherwise how would that work logistically? They'd have to have the perfect match die right at the right time. But then was that person paid? I just didn't want to know. Don't ask, don't tell. But it was hard to keep our relationship from my friends."

Rosie's friends got wind that she was in a long-distance relationship, although they never knew Julian's name or his medical condition. She gave monosyllabic answers to their questions until they stopped asking.

Confidentiality is the con man's friend. It limits knowledge of the con to as few people as possible, keeping law enforcement at bay and reducing the risk of discovery. If a victim keeps quiet, there will be no second-guessing or pointed questions from third parties. What seems perfectly logical to the victim (wiring large sums of money, for example) may raise alarm bells for that person's best friend or family member.

Not every scam requires confidentiality. Some, like investment schemes or affinity fraud, rely on word of mouth to draw in additional victims. For them, publicity helps rather than hinders the scam. These tend to be the multimillion-dollar fraud schemes that affect hundreds or even thousands of people. Perpetrators of these large-scale swindles possess a special kind of hubris. The smaller scams targeting individuals or families are more likely to involve demands of confidentiality because the scammers, like foxes in the henhouse, hope to be in and out with their loot before the chickens raise the alarm.

STRINGING YOU ALONG

Monday, the day of Julian's planned departure, came and went. He had warned Rosie that he might be difficult to contact while he was away, but he promised to check in when he could. His first opportunity came on Wednesday, when he e-mailed her to say he was in the hospital and that the transplant had been scheduled for Friday. It was a brief message, but Rosie found it reassuring.

The next day, he called. The line was clear and he sounded well. Rosie asked him about Thailand. He said it was hot and rainy at the same time. The hospital was comfortable and the Harvard-trained doctor seemed on the ball. Then, sounding apologetic, he said there was one more thing.

"They needed more money. It was going to be an additional $10,000. There were some fees they'd forgotten to include in their quote, something to do with anesthesia and the kind of nurse that would be in the operating room. I wasn't overjoyed about it, but I wasn't going to refuse him now, when he was practically under the scalpel. He asked me to wire the money to his account in New York and he'd be able to access it online from Thailand. I said I'd do it as soon as I got off the phone. I said, 'You owe me for this.' He said, 'The honeymoon's on me.' That was the first time he'd ever made any reference to marriage. I wished him good luck for the operation and then he was gone."

The Conjurer, a painting by 15th-century Dutch artist Hieronymus Bosch, depicts a magician performing the ancient cups and balls trick. At the front of a small gathering of spectators, one man is particularly captivated by the sleight of hand. He leans forward, nearly bent in half, as he inspects the magician's hands. Meanwhile, a pickpocket standing behind the spectator is nimbly lifting a bag of coins from the man's belt.

In this scene, Bosch captures the major elements central to a con. The magician's performance tells a story. With the promise of entertainment and mystery, the magic draws in the spectator. The routine is spellbinding, and while the man's attention is misdirected, the accomplice steals his money. When the performance ends, the crowd disperses. The victim continues to be mystified as he contemplates the magician's skill. Sometime later, he will reach for his coin purse and find it has disappeared as completely as the magician and his props. How long will it take for him to realize he has been robbed? Will he ever know how it was done?

DISILLUSION

As Rosie waited for good news from Thailand, she busied herself with schoolwork and menial tasks. For the first time in months, she visited the reunion site through which she had first made contact with Julian. It had grown significantly in size since the last time she had seen it. One of the new additions was an "In Memoriam" page for alumni who had passed away. She clicked on it. As she scrolled through the names and pictures, she saw familiar faces, a few of whom had died while they were still in high school. Some of the more recent deaths were news to her. Then she saw one name that caused her to shriek aloud: Julian's.

"My first thought was, oh my god, he's dead. The transplant failed. But how did that news make it onto the site before I found out myself? I was confused. But then I took a closer look at the listing and it said he had died the previous year in a car accident. That couldn't be right."

Rosie searched for the obituary online and found it. The Julian she had gone to high school with had indeed perished in a car accident, in Des Moines, Iowa, where he served as a pastor at the United Methodist Church. There was even a photo of him with his family, a wife and three children. The obituary mentioned his high school.

Her mind reeled. If that was Julian from high school, then who on earth was on the operating table?

"That's what I was thinking. Who is getting a liver transplant in Thailand? It took a good few hours before it dawned on me that perhaps no one was getting a liver transplant. There was no Julian, so maybe the whole thing was a ruse. It seems obvious now, but it really wasn't at the time. I was still waiting for his call, but I started to panic because I didn't know what I would say to him. I felt sick to my stomach."

But the call never came. Rosie thinks that Julian had played out his hand. Maybe he had found another target. If she hadn't found out the truth, she might have assumed that he died. She would have mourned and moved on.

Every scam will culminate in a discovery phase, where the victim finds he or she has been conned. Discovery is accompanied by a series of emotions ranging from shock, anger, and embarrassment to despair and depression.

At first Rosie thought she could track him down. She went to the police and made a report, but all she had was a cell phone number, now disconnected, and an e-mail address, which was untraceable. She didn't know where he lived in New York or even *if* he lived in New York. She didn't know his real name. She gave the police a description and the one photo she had of him. It was a photo of the two of them taken during the trip to New York. It showed the couple in Central Park, his face partially obscured by her hair.

"It took me a long time to grasp the extent to which I'd been duped. I had to go back and look at everything he'd ever told me and accept that it was all a lie. Even if some details had been true, like maybe he had a daughter in California, it didn't matter, because it was all just feeding the greater lie, which was that he was Julian, he was dying, and he loved me. All my mother's money is gone, plus additional money I withdrew from my savings. A total of $75,000."

Rosie fell prey to a con known as the sweetheart scam, in which singles are targeted by con artists who use romance as a means to empty their accounts. It was also an affinity scam, utilizing a shared identity as alumni from the same high school to accelerate the bonding process.

Cons are theft combined with deception, and the variations are infinite. They range from relatively brief encounters on the sidewalk to cross-continental swindles lasting months or even years. Throw in an arrest warrant, a relative in distress, or sudden wealth, and their lure becomes ever more irresistible. A confidence game is a specific kind of scam in which victims place their confidence or trust in the perpetrator, only to be betrayed, as Rosie was.

When opportunities present themselves, con artists are quick to act. They keep a close watch on current events. War, recession, high unemployment, foreclosures, natural disasters—the worse the news is, the more the con artist has to work with. As practitioners of the art of manipulation and deception, they appeal to the entire range of human emotions and are good at what they do. Perpetrators may have access to personal information about the victim that makes their stories more credible. The man masquerading as Julian had done his homework. He had researched the high school, found the reunion site, probably done a background search on Rosie. No doubt he e-mailed several female alumni and waited to see who would respond.

Scams are loosely constructed. They are built on quicksand and will collapse under too much scrutiny. There are several points throughout the relationship at which Rosie could have exposed Julian for the fraud he was, if she had demanded more verification of his identity, of his illness, of his business or history. Caution is paramount in any dealings with strangers or where money is involved. Because the purpose of a con is to get money under false pretenses, there will always come a point at which the subject of money comes up. And because we live in a highly technical age when we are linked to our money through various forms of identification (bank account numbers, credit cards, Social Security numbers) and electronically (PINs, passwords, online banking), attempts to access your personal information are equivalent to demands for cash.

If the conner approaches you, whether through an e-mail, a knock at the door, or in the produce section at the grocery store, there will be signs to watch for. Julian's con took place over the course of months and netted him $75,000, but a con can also be condensed into a matter of minutes and still exhibit the same characteristics.

Rosie still works as a teacher in North Carolina. Her experience with Julian has left her skittish. She no longer participates in her high school's alumni site and limits her online activity to reading news headlines and browsing for recipes. She makes it a rule to correspond only with close friends and family.

"I've found it comforting to stick to familiar routines. I socialize with a small group of people I've known for years. We do the same three or four things, go the same places. It's hard to imagine ever dating again. I just want to hole up in my house. A friend of mine asked me if I was suspicious at any point along the way. Honestly, I wasn't. It's only with hindsight that certain things seem fishy. When you're in the middle of it, it just feels like life, and I never expected to run into someone who would go to so much trouble to rip me off. I never imagined that such a person existed. I told my friend that if I'd been given the choice, it would have been so much easier to write Julian a check at the outset, to take the financial hit and not have to endure the emotional distress."

For the first few months after it happened, Rosie was apprehensive that Julian might turn up again. He knew where she lived and worked. He was familiar with the most intimate details of her life. For whatever reason, he didn't make any further contact. With no hope of identifying or apprehending him, law enforcement hit a dead end. Without any form of closure, Rosie was left with conflicting emotions. On one hand, she was deeply wounded and devastated. On the other hand, she still wrestled with a residual yearning for the good times she had shared with Julian.

"One of the things that made the whole betrayal so impossible to comprehend at first was that Julian had never been unpleasant to me in any way. On the contrary, he'd always been absolutely chivalrous, sensitive, and likeable. I never saw his dark side. Aside from robbing me of my life savings and shredding my faith in humanity, Julian was a pretty nice guy."

(3)

THE WEAKEST LINK

Why Scams Work

Trey remembers one of the first cons he ever pulled. When he was in high school, his older sister April worked as a pediatric nurse. On her frequent visits home, she shared with her family stories of life on the pediatric ward. She spoke of the generosity shown toward sick children, particularly the terminally ill. There were constant donations of food, entertainment, and other treats to keep the kids' spirits up. One local car dealership paid for a daylong outing at an amusement park. A dentist's office funded a monthly birthday party for long-term patients. A local clown came in regularly to hand out balloon animals.

Where others might see heartwarming beneficence, Trey saw opportunity. He lifted his sister's hospital ID badge, scanned it, and made a passable copy, replacing her name and photo with his own. He then went to a neighborhood on the wealthier, far side of town and began knocking on doors to solicit donations for sick children. The response surpassed his expectations.

"I made sure to dress well, in khakis and a button-down shirt. I had the ID card around my neck. I had a clipboard with a form on it. People could write down their contact information to get a formal thank you from the hospital. I had printed out receipts like the kind you get at Goodwill when you donate stuff."

The hours spent listening to his sister's stories paid off. Trey was able to relate in detail the kind of treatments terminally ill children have to endure, the pain they suffered, and the emotional toll exerted on both the patients and their families. He explained how every contribution made would directly impact and improve the children's lives.

"Some people don't answer their door. Fine. But if you've taken the time to come to the door and open it, you're probably not going to just slam it shut in my face immediately. You'll let me at least say who I am and what I'm doing there. That's all the time I needed."

Trey figured that if he got caught or questioned, he could say he really was trying to raise money for the hospital and claim a connection through his sister. But no one questioned his credentials. He made $500 in one morning, enough to convince him that he had a talent for deception. Trey quit his part-time job at a fast food restaurant.

Con artists are master storytellers. A complete lack of conscience means that they are willing to use any tools at their disposal to cheat their victims. This includes sharp instincts and a keen practical understanding of human psychology.

After just one outing, Trey was able to recognize differing reactions to his pitch and adjust his approach slightly, depending on the reaction. One group of residents exhibited immediate sympathy.

"Their eyes would get a little misty. They'd shake their heads and make comments about how sad it all was. Those people gave out of compassion. Whether or not they were parents themselves, they could relate to the stories and found them moving. The second group gave out of guilt, guilt because maybe they were doing so well and these poor kids and their families clearly weren't. Or guilt that they didn't really care as much as they should. Or maybe a bit of both. They just wanted this unpleasantness off their doorstep and they could pay to have it go away."

One of the myths surrounding cons is that only certain people get scammed. While there are groups that may be more attractive to con artists simply because of their added vulnerability, the reality is that anyone can be the victim of a scam.

The police never intercepted Trey's charity con, and he went on to make thousands more dollars with it before moving on to more sophisticated and profitable scams. While compassion and guilt helped him land his first score, he soon discovered that there were even more formidable emotions to be tapped.

BASIC NEEDS

For every con, there is a corresponding trait in human nature that is being targeted. Borrowing from psychologist Abraham Maslow's hierarchy of needs, it is not difficult to see how con artists are able to succeed. Maslow's model identifies five levels of needs common to human beings. The most basic needs are physiological, the need for food and water to sustain us, for physical comfort and shelter. Next is the need for safety and security, whether it be economic, physical, or emotional. The third is a need for belongingness and love, or attachment. The fourth is the need for esteem, which can be associated with power, prestige, position, or whatever brings a feeling of self-worth and validation. The highest level of need in Maslow's hierarchy is the need for self-actualization, for living to one's full potential.

A quick glance at some popular cons shows how directly they are linked to one or more of the needs. Money allows us to fulfill our most basic need for sustenance. Without it, we cannot survive. People also seek wealth for other purposes. They require money for economic and physical security, to boost their self-worth, to gain prestige and public recognition. As a result, schemes such as Ponzis, pyramids, boiler rooms, prize notifications, and lottery jackpots thrive. We also need to conserve the money we do have, so anything that purports to save us money is appealing.

For months, Natalia had been meaning to have the dent in her car fixed. The very sight of it brought back bad memories. Leaving work after a heated argument with her boss, she had reversed into a brick wall, causing a substantial indentation in her bumper. Shortly afterward, she lost her job as a paralegal. With estimates of $2,000 or more to have the bumper fixed, and fresh out of a job, Natalia decided to put off the repair until her finances improved. In the meantime, every time she looked at the car, it reminded her of a job she had hated and a boss who made her life hell.

One day as she was out shopping, a man approached her in the parking lot. "He introduced himself as Isaiah. He'd noticed the dent in my car and wanted to give me a free estimate on having it repaired right then and there. At first I said I wasn't interested, but he kept on talking. He said he was from an auto repair company, Fix-it. The name sounded vaguely familiar. He said they had a mobile unit that went around fixing cars on site. He pointed out another man nearby who he said was his partner. The second man was working on a black Lexus."

Natalia asked Isaiah for his card. At first he hesitated, but finally he handed over a card with the company name printed on it, along with someone else's name. Natalia asked him whose card it was. He replied that it belonged to his boss. Figuring she had nothing to lose, she told him to go ahead with the estimate. Isaiah walked around the car and examined the bumper closely for a few minutes. Then he told her he could fix it for $320. She laughed.

"Considering I'd had professional estimates as high as $4,000, this seemed too good to be true. I told him so."

Isaiah said that they were able to charge so little because they had no overhead. All the tools were in his truck and he could be finished by the time Natalia was done with her shopping. If she was not satisfied with the work, she could just call the number on the card and someone would come out at no additional charge. Again he pointed to his partner working on the Lexus.

Still, Natalia was not convinced. She said she'd think about it.

"I went into the store and used my phone to look up the company. It was a legitimate company with good reviews. They did have franchise locations in my area. Then I called my father to ask his opinion. What really sold him was the fact that I'd seen the partner working on another car. In fact, as I was on the phone, I saw a woman approach the Lexus and talk to the guy working on it. I assumed she was the car's owner. My dad said since I'd confirmed the company was legitimate and they appeared to be fixing a car at that very moment, he didn't see any problem with it. With that vote of confidence, I went back out to Isaiah."

Natalia told him she wanted to go ahead. She managed to negotiate a lower price, $280, in exchange for cash payment upon completion of the job. In keeping with her legal training, she had Isaiah write down exactly what he intended to do to her car and sign it. Then she went off to shop.

"When I came back, he was just finishing up. The whole bumper was covered with a thick layer of some kind of dark shiny substance."

Isaiah described the substance as a setting compound that needed to stay on overnight. Natalia was dubious, but he insisted that once the compound was removed, the bumper would be as good as new. He reminded Natalia that she could call if there were any problems.

"I wasn't thrilled, but I thought that once I got the stuff off the bumper, it would look better. It was a great big dent, and even if it wasn't quite as good as new, I would have been happy, given the price."

Natalia paid Isaiah and left. She didn't get around to cleaning off her bumper until a few days later. When she did, she was in for a surprise.

"Not only was the dent still there, but he'd inflicted additional damage on my bumper. I tried calling the number he'd given me, but there was no answer. Then I called the Fix-it number on the website. The person I spoke to said they'd been receiving a lot of calls from people just like me who had been scammed. I felt like a complete fool. I was out $300 and my car was now going to cost even more to fix. I went over it again and again in my mind. There were a lot of red flags, but I thought I'd done my due diligence. I told the Fix-it woman that if they'd put a notice on their homepage alerting consumers to the fact that this scam was being perpetrated, it would probably help a lot of people avoid it. If I'd seen a warning when I went on their site, I would have walked away immediately. Now when I look at my car, I'm reminded of two unpleasant episodes in my life."

Natalia is a highly educated, well-traveled, intelligent person. She's independent and sensible, not given to foolish or risky behavior. The experience of being scammed was traumatic and humiliating. She wonders if she would have been as receptive to the con if she had been employed and more financially stable.

Feeling safe and secure means having a job. It means not being in trouble with the law. It means being debt free. It means having a home and money in the bank. There are cons that attack each one of these concerns. Employment scams promise people jobs but leave them high and dry. Official letters threaten imprisonment and fines if fees are not paid. Scams that offer to clear debt, clean up credit, and reduce mortgage payments use fear to entrap victims.

Fear is a useful tool for swindlers because fear is a great motivator. It can be used to exploit our strong bonds of friendship and family. Protecting our loved ones is always a priority. If we fear they are in danger or hurt, we will act first and ask questions later. Our need for attachment and love binds us indelibly to our loved ones. Con artists know that parents love their children unconditionally and will do anything for them, especially when they are in danger. The phony crisis call is based on this assumption. Another genre of con has been built around the love and generosity that grandparents exhibit for their grandchildren.

The need for belonging causes us to seek out those who are like us and attribute to them a certain amount of integrity based on our shared characteristics or circumstances. Familiarity can lull us into a false sense of security. This is the basis for a category of scams known as affinity fraud. Imagine a new immigrant adrift in a sea of unfamiliar language, customs, and geography who is attempting to navigate an alien and at times unfriendly landscape. Along comes someone who speaks his or her language, has traveled the same road, and knows the ropes. That person offers aid, friendship, and an opportunity that seems too good to pass up.

A number of swindles exploit the need to love and be loved. These sweetheart scams prey on those looking for love and companionship. Nearly everyone who has ever been in a romantic relationship can recall feeling irrational at one point or another, and possibly even acting irrationally. Giving financial support to someone you love and with whom you hope to share a future does not seem particularly extraordinary, and yet, in a sweetheart scam, that is exactly what takes place.

Technology makes it easy for scammers to initiate relationships online from next door or from halfway around the world. A study by the Pew Internet and American Life Project finds that one in 10 adult Internet users in the United States has personally visited an online dating site. Their intentions may be casual or serious, but they are looking to meet someone. Whatever their expectations, they are temporarily fulfilled when they encounter the sweetheart scammer. If they have been doing it for a while, they have probably already made contact with and discounted a number of possible partners. The sweetheart scammer will tailor his or her approach to meet the victim's requirements.

The fifth need Maslow describes is a need for self-actualization, which translates into our grander vision for our lives. What do we hope to accomplish? What are we really capable of? Scams that speak to this need are aspirational in nature.

From a young age, Collette had had a passion for writing. Her third grade poetry booklet, featuring an original haiku on her favorite food, ice cream, was a treasured possession. In high school, she was editor of the literary anthology, to which she contributed lengthy poems reflecting her teenage angst. By the time she headed off to college, she had decided to pursue writing as a career. In her first semester at school, she spotted a classified ad in the student newspaper calling for submissions to a poetry contest. There was no entry fee and poets were free to submit as many poems as they liked of 30 lines or less. The grand prize winner would receive a cash prize, and semifinalists would be published in a poetry anthology.

Collette jumped at the opportunity. She had notebooks full of poetry but had never been published and was curious to know how her writing would be received. She chose five of her shorter poems, typed them up, and sent them off. Two weeks later, she received a response by mail. As she started to read the letter, she shrieked and began again, reading it aloud to her roommate. It was a letter congratulating her on being selected as a semifinalist. All five of her poems would be published in the anthology. Collette was overjoyed. For a moment, she felt the warm glow of validation. She was a real writer. She was going to be published.

Enclosed in the envelope was a second page that quickly dampened her enthusiasm. It was an order form for the published anthology. The first copy, billed as the "original author's copy," would cost her $34.95. Each additional copy was priced at $25.

"I was instantly deflated. I felt like someone had paid me the highest compliment and then immediately punched me in the gut. I wasn't a great poet after all. They just wanted to make a buck off me. Or many bucks, as the case may be. The great irony of it is that if I'd had the money, I probably would have ordered a copy. I wanted to be a writer. I wanted to be published."

Scams like this are not unique to publishing. They exist in every industry in which the eager hopefuls are many and the truly successful are few. This includes modeling, acting, and singing.

INDUCEMENTS

For every trap, there must be bait. Everyone either wants something or wants to avoid something. The carrot or stick element of a con dictates that people must be drawn in by either positive or negative means.

Money is a powerful inducement to action. From minimum-wage workers struggling to make ends meet to jet-setting executives, we are all susceptible to its appeal. David Mamet's film *The Spanish Prisoner*, the story of an elaborate con, contains the prescient line, "A fella said we must never forget that we are human and as humans we must dream and when we dream, we dream of money."

As his criminal career progressed, Trey capitalized on this yearning for a better life. One of his scams involved calling people to tell them they had been left money by a mysterious benefactor. He focused on groups of people likely to come into contact with large numbers of people on a daily basis, such as postal workers and librarians. He called them up, identified himself as an estate lawyer, and told them they had been left a significant sum of money. Incredulity was the usual first reaction.

"They would ask me to repeat the name of the person who left them the money. It didn't matter what the name was. Let's say it's Louise George. They'd usually say they didn't know anyone by that name. I told them they must have made an impression on her, because she'd left them $100,000. Sometimes they told me I had the wrong person. I'd ask, 'Are you Arnie Mason of 1608 Cherry Tree Lane? Have you ever been a postal worker?' They'd respond affirmatively. In that case, there can be no mistake."

Sometimes the individuals would ask for a description of Louise George, searching their memory banks for some connection. Trey had a stock response. "Maybe you were always nice to her, maybe you went out of your way for her and she wanted to remember you. Rich people are eccentric. Whatever her motives, the fact remains, this lady left you money. My job is to make sure you get it."

Trey went on to explain that there was some legal paperwork involved and that the inheritance would be taxed. After bombarding the person with legal jargon, he would offer two options. Either the recipient could take care of all the paperwork and taxes on his or her own, or Trey could do it. Then the beneficiary could just pocket the money and get on with his or her life. Usually the victim was happy to let Trey take care of the bureaucratic red tape.

"Then I'd mention, as an afterthought, that because of the way the law worked, the inheritance had to be paid in whole. I couldn't deduct the taxes or any other fees from the inheritance money. Arnie Mason would have to pay me directly. But he'd still be up $85,000. That's a college education for a grandchild, or a mortgage paid off, or several trips around the world."

For the majority of the population, the notion of becoming wealthy is nothing more than a distant desire. So when someone comes along and insinuates that the unattainable is within reach, it is only natural to become excited. The possibility alone can elevate our heart rates. Anyone who has bought a lottery ticket knows this feeling. The interval between buying the lottery ticket and checking the winning numbers is a period in which anything is possible. That is the feeling a con artist wants to cultivate, that feeling of possibility, of excitement, that momentum that keeps you hooked.

Trey made it sound easy and convincing. Wire him the $15,000 immediately and he would pay the taxes and process the paperwork. Then he would overnight a check for $100,000. As he guided his victims through the steps, Trey chatted with them about family and work. He said that informing beneficiaries was the best part of his job. He had ready answers to all their questions and spoke authoritatively. His attention to detail made his spiel more believable. The check would have to be signed for. They should plan to be at home the morning it was scheduled to arrive. By the time he was done talking, their excitement was palpable.

One quality that many con artists draw on is their natural charm or charisma. Scams that rely on personal interaction require the crooks to win over their targets, also known as marks. In order to do so, they have to possess a degree of persuasiveness that draws the marks in and convinces them to comply with whatever requests the swindler eventually makes.

A scammer knows that people, although gifted with the capacity for reason, are often led by their emotions. Con artists use this to their advantage, playing on human emotions such as fear, hope, greed, and compassion. They craft their approaches to speak directly to our greatest aspirations or our deepest fears. Logically, people know their chances of winning a lottery are slim to none. But when that jackpot notification comes, there's a part of them that thinks they've finally caught that lucky break. Hope springs eternal.

Sifting fact from fiction and recognizing the ways in which we make ourselves emotionally and psychologically accessible to con artists are the first steps to avoiding their advances.

VULNERABILITIES

Con artists have existed throughout history. They thrive because we have become no less vulnerable to the scams they perpetrate. While we have developed sophisticated systems for securing our buildings and vehicles, and keep our money in impenetrable vaults, none of this provides an adequate defense against con artists.

We are the weak link. Although our technology has advanced light years, as human beings we remain creatures of sentiment. Our emotions can be manipulated, in many cases quite easily. Advertisers know it. Politicians know it. Conners certainly know it.

Sometimes the very attributes we think make us impervious to con artists are the same ones that lead to our downfall. Take for example the online IQ test. We've all seen those ads in the corner of the screen that tease us with multiple-choice questions or invite us to test our wits against friends who have supposedly already taken the test. Maybe we're feeling competitive or maybe we're curious to know just how smart we are. The point is that no one who completes an online IQ test is doing so because they think they're unintelligent. Unfortunately, such tests can be a front for cell phone scams. The user takes the test, keys in a mobile phone number to receive the score, and later discovers that he or she has been charged for services or downloads unwittingly authorized. By appealing to ego, these unscrupulous marketers know they will elicit a response from people who would describe themselves as smart and technically savvy.

We all want to provide for ourselves and our families. When someone comes along with a shortcut to wealth, happiness, or success, we want to believe. Even in a cynical age, people retain a measure of optimism. In some cases, we are greedy. Something for nothing sounds like a good deal. We forget our parents' admonition that there's no such thing as a free lunch.

People are compassionate. A damsel in distress or a hard-luck story will always get our attention. As Trey's hospital scam demonstrated, helping others gives us a sense of satisfaction and makes us grateful for our own relative good fortune. Con artists recognize these feelings as a form of weakness and are quick to exploit them. If the victim is in a weakened or vulnerable state, the swindler can also fill a void in that person's life.

Harry was at the bank. It was the end of the week, and he was the last person in a very long line. As he waited, he started up a conversation with the woman in front of him. They commiserated over the length of the line and talked about their weekend plans. She had left work early and was planning a big weekend with her son, who would be celebrating his fifth birthday. Looking at her watch, she said she hoped the line would move quickly. She had to cash a check and get to the party supply store. Harry nodded. He had three grandchildren and knew how important birthdays are to kids. A couple of minutes passed. The woman smiled and talked about the Spider Man cake she ordered for her son. Another glance at her watch. Then she had an idea. Was there any way Harry could cash the check for her? The check was for $120, but she offered to take less just to get out of the line. Did Harry have any cash on him? He hesitated for a moment before agreeing. He pulled out his wallet and handed her $120, saying he hoped her son would have a happy birthday. She endorsed her check over to him, thanked him profusely, and quickly left the bank.

It wasn't until a week later that he received the check back in the mail with a note saying it was counterfeit. The account number was nonexistent.

Harry wasn't sure what to make of the situation. "Either she's something close to what she says she is, a mother who's having a hard time making ends meet. Or she's a hardened criminal, a complete liar who goes from bank to bank running this scam. I prefer to think of her as down on her luck and desperate, because then maybe this money I gave her really did help pay for a little boy's birthday. I know that's not realistic, but to think of her the other way, I don't want to live in that kind of world."

Harry's reaction to being robbed demonstrates the traits that made him an ideal victim. The woman who fleeced Harry used the story of

her child to engage him. It's not a stretch to imagine that stories involving children would elicit sympathy from most people. She probably
also made use of the art of cold reading to push Harry's buttons. Cold
reading is the skill of divining information about a stranger by taking
into account their gender, age, body language, appearance, mannerisms,
speech, carriage, and any other readily identifiable features. Cold reading is the ability Sherlock Holmes displays when describing people's
lives in great detail after a single encounter.

For a scam artist, cold reading is extremely useful in determining
how to customize a scam. Take the bank setup. Harry is a senior citizen.
He wears a wedding ring. Immediately the con artist can make some
assumptions about him. He is or was married, so he's likely to have children, and based on his age, grandchildren. He is retired, so he has time
to stand in line at the bank. Because he grew up in an era where mothers
didn't work outside the home, he will feel sorry for this working mother.
He will be courteous and want to help. She may remind him of his
daughter. In a line full of people, Harry is the most attractive candidate.

He is certainly far more attractive than the person standing directly in
front of her, a woman in a suit. One look at her and the con artist knows
that she will not be receptive. She is a career woman in her 30s, no wedding ring, checking e-mail on her smartphone. She is wearing expensive
shoes. A quick read would deduce that this is a woman on her lunch
break, in a hurry to get back to work, single, distracted, self-engrossed.
She probably likes to spend her hard-earned money on herself and is not
likely to help a stranger. She is also fixated on the phone, which doubles
as a "do not disturb" sign.

Because it deals in generalities and stereotypes, cold reading is not
a perfect science. However, it is precise enough to be a powerful tool.
Anybody who has had a palm or tarot card reading and thought the
psychic was scarily accurate has been the subject of a cold reading. One
novice tarot card reader, nervous on her first time out, was advised to remember one cold reading truism: "Women want to know about relationships; men want to know about money. And if it's a woman, remember
to say something about her father issues."

Longtime scam merchant Trey, of the fake charities and inheritances,
offers his take on why his and other cons are successful. "Why do people
fall for scams? Maybe they're greedy or lonely or desperate or needy or

afraid or generous or selfish or bored. Or maybe they believe they deserve a lucky break. It's like asking why people fall in love. They fall in love because they're people and that's what people do. If you're human, you can't control the way you feel. But you can control the way you act."

After Natalia's experience with the Fix-it flimflam, she felt pretty low. "I was so angry, but part of the anger was directed at myself. I should have known better. I tried to think about what made me go for it, because I did have doubts. In the end, there were little things that convinced me. It was the partner working on the other car. It was the business card with the company name on it. It was the fact that he said they would accept a check if I wanted to pay that way. And then I went online and everything seemed fine. At any stage, I might have figured out the truth, if I'd called the real Fix-it office or searched for 'dent scam.' But I think a part of me wanted to believe it was true. I badly wanted to fix my car. It had been bugging me for months. I didn't want to spend a fortune to do it. Then here comes Isaiah offering me a way to kill two birds with one stone. Was it too much to hope for that I would catch a break? I guess it was."

All the qualities that make us unique and complex beings also open us up to risk. In other words, we feel, therefore we fall. Protecting ourselves can mean second-guessing our emotions and reactions. It's not pleasant to consider the prospect that someone's intentions may be nefarious, but it is prudent. And in the long run, any unpleasantness we experience in the name of prevention will be far less painful than what we would have to endure as a scam victim.

(4)

MAYHEM IN THE MAIL

Avoiding Postal Pitfalls

Carl is a geologist, a man of science. He describes himself as a rational person, governed by reason and logic. He doesn't gamble, not even in a friendly game of cards with friends. He has lived in the same Arizona town for 15 years. It is a comfortable and uneventful existence. Or at least it was, until the day he received what he thought was good news.

"I usually go through the mail in the evening, when I'm watching television. There's so much junk mail these days. It's either junk or bills, so I'm on autopilot for the most part. Then I came across something that looked a little unusual. It had foreign stamps on it. I think they were British. Anyway, they were real stamps, which is what caught my eye."

The letter informed Carl that he was the lucky third-place winner in a European lottery drawing. Everything was laid out in great detail. The lottery was a collaboration between several members of the European Union, with the participants' names drawn at random from Europe, Asia, and North America.

"I remember there was a disclaimer at the bottom of the letter, the same kind of thing you see at the bottom of e-mails from lawyers. That made it seem more legitimate to me. It was intriguing, but I didn't immediately respond. I was skeptical too."

Carl put the letter aside, but over the next week, he found himself thinking about it often, in meetings, out in the field, as he drifted off to sleep at night.

"The letter didn't specify an amount, so just for fun, I would speculate on how much it might be and mentally allocate it to various things. If it was $1 million, I would spend so much on the house, so much on a trip, so much on my kids. If it was more, well, that would open up additional possibilities. Ultimately that was what drew me in. I just had to know how much. At that point, it was more a game than anything else. I had nothing to lose."

Carl retrieved the letter, worked up his nerve, and called the "prize payment center" as instructed. Things immediately became more real. Carl recited the identification number provided in the letter and was informed that his lottery winnings totaled $4.8 million. That did not include a tax payment of $85,000 for which he was responsible.

"It was like a roller coaster ride. The lottery official told me $4.8 million and I couldn't help feeling exhilarated. Then he mentioned the taxes and immediately I came crashing back to earth because I don't have that kind of cash lying around. But he obviously anticipated that, because he had a quick fix. He told me the lottery organization had an arrangement with a company in the U.S. that could loan me the money and I could pay them back when I got my winnings."

As Carl saw it, he still had little to lose. He might as well see if the loan money materialized. "It all happened so fast. He took my details and said I could expect a loan check within a few days. They wouldn't even need to run a credit check because obviously they knew I was going to be good for the money."

Three days later, a check for $85,000 arrived in an envelope with a U.S. postmark. Until it came, Carl had still harbored doubts, but after depositing the check into his bank account, he figured it was time to celebrate.

"The amount was credited to my account right away, but I waited a few days to make sure it had cleared. Then I wired the money to London as directed. When I called the prize center to follow up on my payment, the phone had been disconnected."

Although he knew then that the whole episode had been a hoax, it wasn't until his bank contacted him a week later that he realized just how he'd been taken. The loan check was a fraud and he was now liable for the $85,000 he had wired.

"It's hard not to feel like a complete fool," says Carl. "I've always been so careful. For just a moment I let go of that caution, and I'll be paying for it for the rest of my life. As a scientist, I believe in what I can see. And when I saw that check go into my account, I thought that was it."

When Carl discovered he'd been conned and his bank account emptied, he went to the police, who empathized but told him they could not retrieve or even trace his money. Wiring was as good as sending cash, and the money had disappeared overseas. Carl became deeply depressed as he was faced with the prospect of being tens of thousands of dollars in debt. Some weeks later, he was contacted by someone claiming to be from the state district attorney's office.

"The caller said they'd heard I had lost money to a lottery scam. She said that other people had also been affected and that they'd conducted an investigation in cooperation with Interpol. The good news for me was that they'd been able to recover some of the money that was stolen and would be returning a portion to me. Not all of it, but a significant chunk. They just needed my bank details and Social Security number and they'd be able to transfer the money into my account immediately. I wanted to believe her. I really did. But my trust had been shattered to smithereens."

Carl told the woman that he was surprised. The police had told him they would not be able to trace the money. He said he would have to check with his contact in the police department and get back to her. Could he get a phone number?

"As soon as I mentioned the police, she was in a great hurry to get off the phone. She wouldn't leave a number and said she'd call me back. She never did."

Carl's instincts were right the second time around. Con artists like to milk their victims for as much and as long as they can. Once the victims have paid out, they often continue to pay out in the hopes that they will eventually recoup their losses or receive their reward. Tragically, those who are burned once are often put on a "sucker's list," a group of people who are considered easy targets and to whom these con artists come back time and again. The process of returning to a victim to perpetrate another scam is known as *reloading*.

Raymond, a federal law enforcement officer specializing in fraud cases, describes the difficulty of getting into the head of a swindler. "It's almost impossible for a decent, law-abiding person to understand how someone could make a living that way. Normal people have consciences. But not the con man. He doesn't care who he hurts. He doesn't even give it a second thought. Lying, cheating, taking, that's what he's all about. There's no afterthought there. Once he's taken your money, he's on to the next person, unless he can somehow get more out of you."

Carl was the victim of a scam incorporating two widespread forms of mail fraud: the foreign lottery and the fraudulent check. The logistics of this con and others like it rely on precision timing, loopholes in the banking system, and ultimately, the power of persuasion.

Despite the increasing use of e-mail, text messaging, and other forms of communication, paper mail is still going strong. The U.S. Postal Service may handle more than 177 billion pieces of mail in a year. The mail provides easy points of entry for con artists. Mass mailings, forged stationery, false advertising, "guaranteed" riches, and empty threats are all designed to relieve people of their hard-earned cash as quickly as possible with minimal effort.

Prize and lottery scams continue to be among the most common scams perpetrated. Everyone wants to be a winner. Sweepstakes, lotteries, raffles, drawings—from retail outlets to cereal boxes to fast food, it seems that everywhere we go, we are bombarded with opportunities to win something. Swindlers are well aware of the popularity of prize-based competitions and eager to cash in. Bogus prize promotions begin with a notification that you have won something. The prize can be a piece of merchandise, anything from jewelry to electronic equipment to a car. Whatever the prize, you will be required to make a payment, sometimes referred to as a "shipping and handling fee," in order to receive it. In many cases, no prize is ever forthcoming. In some instances, you will receive something, but the value and quality of the item will be far less than expected and certainly less than the amount you paid to collect it.

Closely related are foreign lottery and sweepstakes schemes. These do not involve material prizes but promises of cash winnings. Aside from being a rip-off, the premise itself is illegal. Federal law prohibits taking part in foreign lotteries while you are in the United States.

NICE WORK IF YOU CAN GET IT

Fake checks like the one used to dupe Carl are ubiquitous in the scam business. Because they add an extra semblance of legitimacy to any con, they are useful and versatile. Instead of asking people for money outright, perpetrators can now make it appear that they are giving their marks something in exchange, that the criminals are laying out the money, when in fact the opposite is true.

College student Rebecca was in the market for a part-time job when she received a letter from a company looking for people to evaluate local businesses. It included information specific to Rebecca.

"I'd been paid to do market research before. I participated in a few focus groups, where you give your opinion on various products and top-ics. The letter mentioned the work I'd done for that particular market research company and asked me if I'd be interested in being a mystery shopper. I thought the other company, the real one, had referred me to this mystery shopping company. How else would they have known about the work I'd done? It seemed on the up and up."

As the letter explained, the job was straightforward. The company would provide Rebecca with money to be spent at specific retail outlets. She would shop, report back on her experiences, and keep a small fee for herself. It looked like a win-win scenario, so she e-mailed the company expressing her interest.

"Next thing I know, I receive a check for $4,000, with a list of places they want me to visit and an amount to spend. Some of them were stores and restaurants that didn't even have locations in my state, which I told them. They said not to worry, just to pick three or four of the ones that were nearby. I could wire the excess money back after deducting expenses and a $200 fee for myself. They offered me a bonus if I could do it all by the end of the week. I was excited. Who doesn't want to spend other people's money? I deposited that check right away. I'm a student, remember. My bank balance had never been that high."

The next day, Rebecca began at the local mall, visiting a high-end department store to buy cosmetics. She dutifully noted the store's decor, lighting, ambience, customer service, layout, and ease of navigation. This was followed by a trip to a discount shoe retailer and a video game

store. After working up an appetite, she finished off the evening with a
three-course meal at one of the designated restaurants.

"The sad thing is, I was a good employee. I took it seriously. I was very
organized. I scanned in all my receipts, typed up my notes, and e-mailed
everything to them. They had sent me instructions on where to wire the
leftover money and told me to keep an extra $50 for being so quick. I
did the whole thing online."

Rebecca considered it easy money and was looking forward to another
assignment. She e-mailed the company and got no response but didn't
give it too much thought. Then she received another letter, this time from
her bank, informing her that the check she had deposited was counterfeit.

"It never occurred to me that it could be counterfeit. I had no reason to doubt it. It looked completely real, with a genuine bank's name.
Nobody at the bank questioned it. The funds were showing up in my
account. What more is there?"

The success of fake checks rests on the time it takes a check to complete the circuit from the depositor's bank to the payer's bank. When
Rebecca deposited the check, her bank credited the amount to her account, pending clearance. Within a couple of days, the check appeared
to have cleared and the funds appeared in her bank account. However,
a check does not clear completely until after it has been presented to
the issuing bank and the funds withdrawn from the payer's account. In
her case, when the check was presented to the bank that supposedly issued it, the bank declined payment because it was fraudulent. That bank
notified her bank, which in turn notified her. By the time word reached
Rebecca, the $2,700 she had wired was long gone.

Fraudulent checks often look identical to genuine checks. The key
is to consider the source. Being contacted suddenly by someone either
asking for or offering money should be a tip-off that a scam is waiting
in the wings.

"At first I thought it was a mistake." Rebecca tried contacting the mystery shopping company. The phone number on their letterhead was not
in service and her e-mails and letters went unanswered. With her bills
coming due, and her bank account in the red, Rebecca was forced to sell
her car and cut back on classes in order to find a more reliable job.

"I went back to the legitimate market research company to tell them
what had happened, and they claimed they don't share the names of the

people who do work for them. So maybe it was an inside job? I'll never know." Despite her experience, Rebecca maintains a grim humor about having been conned. "Well, at least I got to keep the shoes. I try to wear them as much as possible. I call them my thousand-dollar shoes. If I'd known I was going to be cheated, I would have bought more."

Real mystery shopping jobs do exist, but mystery shopping and other work-at-home schemes are irresistible to con artists because they are equally appealing to potential victims. The number of people looking for work-at-home jobs is ever expanding, but the pool of jobs that meet the criteria of being flexible, part-time, and off-site is limited. Ads or solicitations that promise good money for minimum effort are guaranteed scams. Envelope stuffing, data entry, medical billing, craft assembly, and rebate processing are some other classic work-at-home scams.

Reshipping is a work-at-home scam that makes victims unwitting accomplices in criminal activity. People apply for positions with titles like "processing assistant" or "merchandising manager." They are asked to receive packages on behalf of their employers and mail them to foreign addresses. The merchandise is stolen or purchased with stolen credit cards. In other cases, they are recruited to help launder stolen money through their bank accounts. In all cases, the shippers are never paid. They are either given phony checks or asked to provide their bank account information for payment, in which case they become victims of identity theft. Furthermore, these victims can be charged by the police for handling stolen goods or participating in money laundering.

IT'S UNCLE SAM

It's difficult to scam someone who needs or wants for nothing. Luckily for con artists, most people do not fit into that category. Finding some motivation, such as fear, greed, or desperation, is essential to a successful con. Mail scams involving officialdom play to both fear and greed and take advantage of the inclination of upstanding citizens to obey authority.

As with fake checks, letters claiming to be from official sources are often difficult to distinguish from the real thing. Adding to the confusion is the fact that scammers are well informed. They keep up with the news. They check the calendar and plan their scams to coincide with other events taking place.

The decennial census is a conner's dream. U.S. residents are required by law to complete a census survey, which in 2010 consisted of 10 questions. Census surveys were mailed in the spring, and households were sent letters beforehand telling them to expect the survey shortly. What better time to send people a form claiming to be from the government, requesting personal information? The Census Bureau had already asked people to provide names, birth dates, and addresses. All the crooks had to do was to ask respondents to provide their Social Security numbers. Those who did soon became victims of identity theft. They include a Pennsylvania mayor whose attempt to do her civic duty by responding promptly led her to divulge her Social Security number. It is not inconceivable that the federal government would ask for a Social Security number; after all, the Internal Revenue Service does every year.

Those who fall victim to official-appearing letters are often ignorant of their rights and entitlements. This allows con artists to spin a story that sounds plausible and contains a ring of accuracy but is in fact a lie.

Nelson and Sonia bought their house in Southern California as newlyweds in 2003, when the housing market was booming. "We bought high, no question," says Nelson. "And a few years later, we watched prices plummet. Luckily for us, we are still able to afford our mortgage, and we live in an area that will always be in high demand."

"And we're not going anywhere anytime soon," adds Sonia.

Still, with the economic downturn, the couple was looking to save money where they could. "It was the end of the year. We had just received our tax bill from the county, and our property tax was a hefty chunk of change, as always. I didn't really think much of it until we got the second letter a week later." The second letter informed the couple that their property may have been overassessed and offered them the opportunity to apply for reassessment.

Sonia brings out the letter. It has the trappings of an official communication. It includes an assessor's identification number. There is a bar code prominently featured in the upper right-hand corner, and the text quotes accurately the current value at which their house is assessed. Also in the letter is a calculation of what their property value could be after reassessment.

"It was considerably lower." She points to another figure. "This is what they said our new property tax figure would be. It's a savings of $1,500."

The letter offered to arrange for a reassessment for a service fee of $180, with a money-back guarantee if their property did not qualify for a reduction in taxes.

"Did it sound expensive?" Nelson shrugs. "Not really, in the scheme of things. We're both busy people, and it seemed worthwhile to have someone do it for us, especially if it was going to save us money in the long run. So we sent off a check."

The check was cashed, but no information was forthcoming, so they called the toll-free number on the letter, which turned out to be the customer service number for a clothing company.

"They just threw any old number on there," says Sonia. "Probably took it off a catalog lying on the kitchen table. I wonder what the bar code was for. Maybe they photocopied it off a soup can."

They finally contacted the county assessor's office and discovered that they could have applied for a property tax reassessment free of charge.

Nelson discovered something else when he called the county. "It turns out that because we bought the house during the bubble, we were entitled to an automatic review of our property taxes and they were reduced automatically. I guess all in all, we were lucky that we weren't taken for more. But now I'm so paranoid. When I got our census form, it looked like the real thing, but I took it down to City Hall just to make sure. Once bitten, twice shy, I guess."

Misleading letters of the sort sent to Nelson and Sonia became so widespread that the California State Assembly passed a law specifically making such solicitations illegal as of January 2010. Although the law is useful in helping to take action against violators, scam artists are by definition not bound by the law or by ethical standards of any sort, and "official" letters persist.

CHAIN, CHAIN, CHAIN

"I remember chain letters from my childhood, but I never thought they'd still be going." Josette is a journalist who answers consumer affairs questions in her weekly newspaper column. "Here's one," she says, pulling a letter out of a manila folder. "A reader sent it in to me. It's two pages, single spaced." She skims the pages. "This is pretty typical."

The letter is full of testimonials by different people claiming to have made six figures following the steps outlined in the letter. "As seen on TV!" is the heading on one page.

"What's interesting is that they assure you here that this isn't a scam. Sometimes they claim the letter has been screened and approved by the postal service. Obviously they expect people to be a little wary."

The instructions are simple enough. They vary from letter to letter, but in this particular instance, there is a list of 10 names. The recipient is told to send $1 to each person on the list, remove the top name on the list, and add his or her own at the bottom. There are even helpful tips on how to retype the list and cut and paste it onto the letter.

"The person is then supposed to make copies of the letter and send it out to a bunch of people in the hopes of stimulating a flood of dollar bills. This one just asks for money, but others are actually selling something, like software or mailing lists. It's an outright scam, not to mention illegal."

Like any pyramid scheme, the originators are the only ones making money, and they rely on their victims to perpetuate the scam by sending out additional letters at their own expense.

Josette understands the appeal of chain letters. "People who are taken in by chain letters are not just people overcome by greed. Sure, they want to make money, and this appears to be an easy way to do it. But beyond that, I think there's an almost folksy quality to chain letters, particularly those that come in the mail. They're old-fashioned. Here's someone supposedly saying give me a buck and we can get rich together. Not only that, but you can help make all these other people rich too. Even if you don't know the other names on the list, you have the feeling of community there. Plus, you can send it to all your friends and family and help enrich them too."

Those who choose to participate by sending money and forwarding the letters are violating federal postal statutes, which considers such chain letters a form of gambling and prohibits them.

"Worst-case scenario, you not only shell out all this money for copying and payment to your chain buddies, but you end up charged with a crime," says Josette. "It's not exactly the happy ending someone has envisioned."

HEY, I DIDN'T ORDER THAT

There's no denying the convenience of mail order, and online shopping has only broadened the horizons of armchair consumers. But scammers also find the mail a convenient option for saddling people with merchandise they never wanted or billing them for services they never requested or received.

There are only two kinds of unsolicited merchandise that are legal: clearly marked free samples and merchandise included in a mailing from a charity soliciting donations (e.g., personalized labels, greeting cards, etc.).

If something arrives in the mail unsolicited, you have no obligation to pay for it. Legally, the recipient can consider the item a gift and keep it. If the package has not been opened, it can be marked "Return to sender" and sent back at no additional cost.

The scam is set in motion when the person receives a bill for the merchandise. Some people assume that if they receive something, even in error, they need to or should pay for it. In fact, billing for unsolicited merchandise is illegal.

"I always liked receiving samples in the mail, especially toothpaste or shampoo, something I could use when I was traveling, which I do often." Vivian is an executive at a major insurance company and a mother of two. "But this was ridiculous."

One day, Vivian returned from work to find a large box of cleaning supplies on her doorstep. "There must have been two dozen bottles of industrial-strength disinfectant in there. It wasn't any product I'd ever seen in the stores, more like something you'd see in an infomercial. I checked the mailing label to see if it had been delivered to the wrong address, but no, it had my name on it. Then I thought it must have been my husband, because he sometimes orders random things. So I called him. He denied all knowledge."

Vivian looked for a company name on the box, but the return address was smudged and illegible. "I kept racking my brain to think who could have sent these to me. I asked my mother, my sisters, my friends, on the off chance that it was a gift of some sort. A weird gift, but you never know. Nobody knew what I was talking about."

The next day, a bill arrived in the mail. It demanded payment of $990. "That's $40 a bottle, plus another $30 for shipping. Wow, that's some miracle cleanser. But the invoice at least had an address and phone number."

Vivian tried calling several times but reached a full voicemail box. Meanwhile, the bills kept coming.

"First they were stamped 'past due.' Then I started getting letters threatening legal action if I didn't pay. Then I got one saying I could return the goods but would have to pay a 50 percent restocking fee. It went on and on. Finally, I just repackaged the box and paid to have it sent back. But that didn't stop the bills. What stopped the bills was that I went to the legal department of my company and asked one of the lawyers if they could draft me a scary-sounding letter threatening them back. The letter said that I would go to the attorney general's office and file a complaint if they didn't cease and desist. Maybe they're not used to getting letters like that, because I heard nothing more after that."

Vivian wondered how things might have been different if they had shipped the goods to a business, rather than an individual. "My company's finance department has dozens of employees. If an invoice like that had landed on one of their desks, it might have been paid. Especially if it was for something like toner or paper, which we order in bulk."

Businesses are hit frequently with bogus invoices for merchandise or services, and large corporations are not the only targets. The Federal Trade Commission charged one group of Canadian-based con artists with swindling small businesses and charities in the United States out of millions of dollars through an invoicing scam that charged them for directory listings that were never requested. When the companies refused to pay, they were harassed and threatened repeatedly.

In the same vein, millions of individuals and organizations with personal and professional websites receive urgent notices telling them their domain names are expiring soon and asking them to renew. Those who do find that they have unknowingly transferred their domains to a new registrar.

Bills and renewal notices are so ubiquitous that many people don't take the time to examine each bill as it comes in, to double check the legitimacy of the charges and question them when necessary.

Ironically, Vivian thinks the cleaner scam would have been more effective if they had not sent the box, but rather simply invoiced her. "Another bill on the stack doesn't stand out as much as 24 bottles of disinfectant. With my busy schedule and the number of bills I receive, I would have been much more likely to pay it if they hadn't gotten my attention first with that huge box of stuff."

SHADES OF GRAY

Straddling the fine line between illegal and unethical is the murky world of *negative options*. Law enforcement officer Raymond calls negative options "tricky, because they're not technically illegal, but they're often misleading or even deliberately deceptive. It's the difference between a sin of commission and a sin of omission. Either way, it's a sin."

Club memberships often operate as negative option plans, particularly if they offer free trial memberships. "Beware of trial offers," says Raymond. "They may look appealing, but unless you cancel by a certain date, thereby exercising your negative option, you will continue to receive and be billed for merchandise, whether you want it or not. For example, you see an ad offering 10 books for a penny. Sounds good. You sign up and give them your credit card number but forget to cancel your subscription before the trial period ends. You're now receiving a monthly cookbook at $30 a pop. Then when you do try to cancel, you're given the run around."

Raymond has also heard of companies enrolling customers in multiple club memberships, so that when they cancel one, they continue to receive goods from the others. "My own cousin signed up for a kids' book club. What they didn't tell her was that buying a certain number of books from that club automatically enrolled her in a second club, which had its own purchase requirements and cancellation policy. She started being inundated with books she didn't want, all of which were charged to her credit card."

Terence, formerly an employee at a direct marketing firm, describes how his company worked in partnership with a bank to entrap its customers. "The bank gave us a list of its customers. We sent checks for $25 to each one, along with a letter that said that the money was to thank the person for being a valued customer. When they deposited the check, they were automatically signing up for membership in a program that could get them discounts for things like cars, travel, and clothing. They had 30 days to cancel their membership. Otherwise, the annual fee would be deducted directly from their bank account."

Asked if the letter clearly explained the consequences of depositing the check, Terence does not reply. He claims he left the firm after his own mother received one of the letters and cashed the check.

Also on the receiving end of the letter were people like Adela, who was pleasantly surprised to receive a check in the mail. A recent immigrant from Eastern Europe, Adela had only just opened her bank account and thought the $25 was a gift for new customers. She thought it was a nice gesture and deposited the money. It wasn't until her rent check bounced the next month that she took a closer look at her bank statement and saw a $115 charge. She questioned the bank about the charge and was referred to the direct marketer.

"I called the company, and they told me it was to pay for membership. I told them I don't want any membership. It is a mistake. They said when I deposit the check in my bank, it means I want to be a member. I said no and I asked them to cancel it because I need to pay my rent. They said it is too late."

Adela thought maybe her imperfect English had caused her to misread or misunderstand the initial letter, but she was not alone. Tens of thousands of bank customers were victimized by the same scam. Unlike Adela, some never even noticed the unauthorized charges and went on to have their memberships renewed the following year.

MISSING MAIL

Mailboxes are easily accessed, and with mail being delivered nearly every day, the pickings are plenty. If a mailbox is not locked, there is nothing to stop a criminal from rifling through the mail and pocketing valuable documents such as bank statements, credit card and utility bills, and insurance papers, all of which can be used to steal identities, damage credit history, and tap into bank accounts. Another tactic is for thieves to submit a change of address form to have mail redirected. If statements, bills, or other pieces of mail that arrive regularly stop showing up, it should raise a red flag.

Mail theft and diversion are precursors to identity theft. This goes for outgoing and incoming mail. (The value of the mail and its manipulation by criminals is discussed in greater detail in chapter 10, which deals with identity theft.)

"A lot of people are away from home during the day," says officer Raymond. "So what's to stop someone opening a mailbox and lifting a credit card or bank statement, an insurance or phone bill? And that's the incoming mail. Never leave outgoing mail in your mailbox. Putting the flag up on your mailbox is like issuing an open invitation to thieves. What do people usually mail? Checks with their name, address, and bank account details on them. Always take mail to the post office, inside if possible. If you're leaving it in the mail drop outside, make sure it's before the last pickup of the day. There have been instances of people breaking into mailboxes outside of post offices, or even inserting plastic bags into the mailboxes to collect the envelopes that people drop off."

RETURN TO SENDER

Sensible computer users have virus protection software that scans their computer systems for malicious programs and malware. Our e-mail programs have filters that help to weed out spam and unwanted messages. But we still receive mail the same way we have received it for 150 years, delivered by mail carriers directly to our homes or post office boxes. There is no person or program to scan our mail for malicious intent or potential harm. That responsibility is ours.

In every case described in this chapter, the individuals involved had a choice, which can be good or bad news. Josette, the consumer affairs journalist, says that scams are doubly hard on victims because they often blame themselves. "I've heard from people who are really beating themselves up because they feel their actions have jeopardized their families' future. I'm talking college funds decimated, defaulting on mortgages, having to take second and third jobs, all because of money lost to con men."

Carl, the geologist who thought he'd won the lottery, expresses a similar sentiment. "The worst part was having to tell my wife just how much money we'd lost. That killed me."

As Carl's experience demonstrates, even cautious, rational people can be lured into scams. After analyzing events repeatedly, Carl sees that his downfall was making the call. "The guy was very convincing and had an answer for everything. By the end of the conversation, I felt like if I didn't follow through with it, somebody else would be getting the money, the money that I had come to think of as *my* money. He said delivery was guaranteed and insured by Lloyds of London, which I'd heard of and know to be a legitimate institution. Every time I reflect on it, I think, that's the point at which I could have hung up, that's the point at which I could have turned it around. If I only hadn't called, if I only hadn't agreed to the loan, if only, if only . . ."

Engaging with con artists is dangerous, tricky, and best avoided. The most effective way to dodge a scam is to do so at the outset, to develop a personal firewall. Developing an anti-fraud mindset requires a certain degree of natural suspicion. The intent is not to be overly paranoid but to examine situations with a critical lens, to ask questions before acting, and to view with skepticism any news that comes out of the blue, in particular if it requires you to give up money or personal information. This may mean occasionally erring on the side of caution, but it requires very little effort. And as time goes on, it will become instinctive.

PROTECTING YOURSELF

Be suspicious. If you receive a letter unexpectedly telling you you've won something, assume it's a scam. Shred it immediately. It doesn't matter how appealing it sounds. This applies to any kind of prize notification, whether the promised prize is money, merchandise, or travel.

Do not make contact. Again, shred the letter. Calling a scammer is like a fish putting its mouth on a hook to see what it feels like. Don't give them the chance to reel you in. And they probably will. They're good.

Do not deposit checks from unknown sources. If you receive a check you were not expecting, you can almost be sure it is fraudulent. If the name or circumstances surrounding it are not familiar, or if it has any accompanying correspondence congratulating you on a win, destroy it.

Do not be rushed. One of the telltale signs of a con is the need for speed. If someone sends you a fake check, they need you to deposit it and send them your money before you discover their check is no good. This means they'll want you to work quickly. Hopefully you will never get to this stage because you will have shredded that check.

Never wire money. Con artists prefer wire transfers because they are the equivalent of sending cash; they can be sent worldwide almost instantly.

Do your research. Advertised work-from-home programs are attractive, but most are scams. Beware of any that require you to buy merchandise up front or to send a payment. Also avoid any that guarantee large profits. Even as a legitimate mystery shopper, you will only make between $8 and $20 per evaluation. The Mystery Shopping Providers Association (www.mysteryshop.org) has additional information on locating genuine mystery shopping opportunities.

When in doubt, check it out. If you receive an official-looking letter, don't take it at face value. Mail that looks official but isn't should contain a disclaimer. If there is no disclaimer and the letter is supposedly from a government agency, contact that agency directly. Do not use the contact number provided in the letter. You can find contact information for federal, state, and local government agencies online at www.usa.gov.

Keep it to yourself. Do not reveal personal information to anyone who contacts you out of the blue. Do not reveal personal information to would-be employers unless you are 100 percent confident of their legitimacy.

Lock your mailbox. Mailboxes with locks are available at your local hardware store or big box store.

Hold your mail. If you are leaving town, fill out a hold mail form at the post office or online at www.usps.com. Mail can be held for a minimum of 3 and a maximum of 30 days.

Keep an eye out. If you are expecting a credit card bill or bank statement and do not receive it, contact the institution and make sure they are sending correspondence to the correct address.

Go to the authorities. If you receive something through the mail that seems suspicious or fraudulent, call the U.S. Postal Inspection Service at 1-877-876-2455. You can also file a mail fraud complaint online at their website, https://postalinspectors.uspis.gov.

If you feel the situation is more urgent, or if you have already lost money to a scam artist, contact your local police department. Reporting the crime can help law enforcement officials alert the public and track down the criminals.

(5)

UP CLOSE AND PERSONAL

Danger on Your Doorstep

After renting for more than a decade, Gabriel finally became a home-owner, buying a townhouse in a subdivision outside Nashville. "It was a great feeling. I had the whole house to myself but still felt like I was close enough to my neighbors not to feel isolated. When I moved in, I really enjoyed furnishing the place and doing it up. I felt like I was an adult at last, at the age of 35. Better late than never, right?"

On a Saturday in May, Gabriel was following his usual weekend routine, catching up on household chores and leisurely reading the newspaper. "It was raining, and I remember thinking that it was a perfect day to stay indoors. I had plenty of stuff to do in the morning, and then I was going to spend the afternoon watching a James Bond marathon on TV. It wasn't until about 3 p.m. that I looked outside and thought, wow, it's really coming down."

Gabriel checked the weather reports online and on TV, but there did not appear to be any cause for alarm.

"It was raining when I went to sleep that night and when I woke up the next morning, it had not let up. But this is rain we're talking about. It rains all the time. It wasn't like there was a tornado coming through. It was just rain."

After breakfast, he checked the weather forecast again, and there were no warnings posted for his area. "Every once in a while, I would take a look outside. I could see from my balcony that water was pooling on the grass and was beginning to rush down the streets in a heavy flow. It still didn't worry me until I saw the water begin to creep up my front stoop. After that, things moved pretty quickly."

As Gabriel was assessing the situation, the water rose rapidly. Within minutes, it had seeped under the door and was filling his entryway.

"I kept thinking it would stop, that the water would recede. Instead, it just kept coming and coming. Even as it was happening, I couldn't believe it. When you see your couch floating in water, it just doesn't seem possible. At first I was panicking for my possessions. Then it struck me that I could be in danger if the water didn't stop."

Gabriel went to the garage to see if he could get to his car and drive away, but it was too late. The water in the utility room was already above his ankles, and when he opened the door to the garage, his tires were half submerged.

"I was wading through the water and my mind was just focused on getting to dry ground. The only thing I thought I could do at that point was to go upstairs and hope the water didn't reach that high. So I did. I had visions in my mind of Hurricane Katrina and the people stuck on their rooftops. It was terrifying. The power had gone out, and I sat up there all night in the dark, listening to the water swirling around and lapping against the stairs."

The next day, with his house still flooded, search and rescue teams making their way through Gabriel's neighborhood by boat were able to evacuate him through an upstairs window.

"I got out of there with nothing but the clothes on my back and my wallet. But thank God for those rescuers." Gabriel was taken first to a shelter at a local high school and then caught a ride to a motel that still had a few vacancies.

When the floodwaters eventually receded, Gabriel was faced with the monumental task of assessing the damage to his home and personal belongings and beginning the process of restoration.

"A lot of my possessions were complete write-offs. Not just appliances and clothing and things like that, but stuff that had great sentimental value to me—letters, photos, home videos, books. Shelves had collapsed, wood beams were rotting, cabinet doors were warped and buckled. Walls, floor, furniture, everything was waterlogged and soaked.

The water had gotten everywhere. There wasn't much I could salvage. It took me a while just to come to grips with the devastation. Then I had to think about how to fix it, because I needed somewhere to live. I was thankful to be alive, but being alive meant I had to deal with this situation. And it was overwhelming."

As bad as things were for Gabriel, they were about to get much worse.

A steady stream of contractors showed up in Gabriel's subdivision and on his doorstep, offering help with flood restoration. "All the vans and trucks had out-of-state license plates, some from as far away as Florida and Virginia. My first instinct was to turn them all away and go with a local firm, but all the businesses in the area were too busy. They told me I'd have to wait as long as a month or two. I didn't have that kind of time. I needed to get back into my house. So I started talking to some of the out-of-town guys."

Gabriel went with the ones that seemed the most reliable. "They had a binder with photos of the work they'd done, before and after pictures. The head guy was really sympathetic, said he'd been a flood victim himself. He and his crew were from Texas. They took a look at the house and gave me what I thought was a reasonable estimate, in writing. I signed it and gave them a $500 deposit. I was told it would be better if I stayed out of the house till they were done, since they'd be using dehumidifiers and there would be mold in the air. They were going to rip out the carpets and use a floor-drying mat. They threw a lot of technical terms at me. Okay, fine. I had checked into a motel anyway."

Two days after work was to commence, Gabriel stopped by the house to check on things. What he saw did not instill confidence.

"First of all, it was a mess. There was trash all over the house, fast food containers, pizza boxes, soda cans. They'd put up a ladder in the living room and laid down a tarp. There was a gaping hole in the ceiling of my laundry room that hadn't been there before. The head man was there. I complained about the trash and he laughed and said something like, 'Construction workers, whadaya expect?' He then proceeded to tell me that they'd discovered the damage was even worse than he'd thought, as evidenced by the hole in the utility room. It was going to cost more, and he'd need to buy extra materials. Bottom line was, he wanted another $500."

Gabriel was reluctant, but he was anxious to move back in, and he could see all of his neighbors had crews in fixing their houses. "It's not like I thought this guy was Honest Abe, but I didn't think he was going to cheat me outright. My thinking was, the prices are probably a little inflated, the time frame is probably a little ambitious, but as sad as it sounds, I thought that was pretty much par for the course with home repairs. Plus, I was desperate. All of us were." Gabriel paid the money.

At the end of the week, he returned to find the situation more or less unchanged. "The place still looked like a frat house. They'd ripped out a carpet and moved some of the furniture, but it wasn't anywhere near the progress I'd expected. When I talked to the boss, he was a little less friendly than he had been before. I asked him if he was going to be able to finish by our agreed deadline. He said no, probably not, and then asked for more money, $1,500 this time."

When Gabriel asked what the money was for, the contractor said he needed to rent a dumpster to dispose of the damaged furniture and other items. He also had to apply for a permit to complete some of the work necessary on the house.

"I told him I'd need to see some improvement on the house before I handed over any more money. Then he got kind of nasty. He said he couldn't continue the work until he had the money. He said the agreement I signed required me to pay expenses as needed, and while I was at it, he'd take the money in cash. It was all getting a little heavy, and I felt I needed to get out of the house, so I told him I'd go to the bank and get the money. I wasn't really sure what to do at that point. I definitely was uncomfortable with the idea of handing over any more cash."

Gabriel went to the nearest police station and explained his situation to the officer on duty. "The officer was very helpful. She said they'd had tons of complaints about contractors since the flooding ended. Most of the companies from out of state weren't legally licensed to operate in Tennessee. A lot of them were just fly-by-night operations that were out to swindle folks. She offered to send someone out to the house right there and then, just to check the guys out. I was so relieved."

Accompanied by a uniformed officer, Gabriel returned to his house only to discover that the contractors had gone. "We did a walkthrough of the house. I told the officer that they must have returned to wherever they were staying. He kind of chuckled. I asked him what he was laughing at. He said by the looks of it, they had been staying there in my house and had probably skipped town. It was possible they had followed me, and when they saw I was headed for the police, they hightailed it out of there. So I had lost a thousand dollars, my house was in worse condition than before, there was still no help on the horizon, and I'd had criminals squatting in my house. I just hoped they wouldn't come back. I changed all the locks immediately."

Shady contractors make a habit of following news of extreme weather around the country. They are often found in the wake of natural disasters or severe weather, when they know people will be in need of extensive home repairs. Gabriel eventually found a reputable contractor and had the work done, although it took months to make the house habitable.

Meanwhile, his neighbors Kiki and Etienne were being hit by another door-to-door scam that thrives in post-catastrophic conditions. When the hurricane was declared a federal disaster, area residents were assured that they would be receiving assistance from the Federal Emergency Management Agency (FEMA).

"We're from the Caribbean, so we had been through a few hurricanes in our lives," says Kiki. "The damage was bad, but we were told that FEMA was on the case. Sure enough, a guy showed up on our doorstep while we were salvaging some belongings. He said he was from FEMA; he was wearing the FEMA jacket you always see on TV. He had a badge and a form for us to fill out, to apply for disaster relief. The form asked for name, address, Social Security number, asked us for our insurance information, household income. I remember I looked across the way, and in the distance I could see another person wearing a FEMA jacket standing in the doorway of another house. It looked like they were going to every home in the neighborhood. Seeing that was reassuring to me."

The man told the couple they could either complete the form on the spot or keep it and mail it in at their convenience. However, filling it out immediately would expedite the release of federal funds to help with their repairs and temporary housing.

Etienne asked him why they were going door to door. "He said that a lot of people were displaced and didn't have access to their computers and other forms of technology that would help them find the FEMA information, so they wanted to bring the information to us. Kiki filled out the form while the man waited. We gave it to him and he started walking away."

Then, almost as an afterthought, the man turned around and came back with an additional piece of paper. He said he had forgotten to mention that they could either have their check mailed or have the funds electronically deposited into their account. He warned that requesting a check would take longer, given the bureaucracy at FEMA and the fact that mail service had been disrupted by the weather.

After a quick discussion, Kiki and Etienne agreed that electronic transfer sounded far more convenient, so they signed an authorization form providing their bank account information. They were not alone; dozens of homeowners in their complex did the same.

A few days later, Gabriel stopped by and spoke to Etienne. "He asked if we'd heard the news about the guys going around. I assumed he meant the contractors, so I said that I had, because he'd told us his story, and we'd heard similar things from some of the other neighbors. He said, 'No, I mean the FEMA guys.' It turns out they had nothing to do with FEMA. They were just crooks trying to get at people's personal information so that they could mess with our bank accounts and our good names."

At first it was unclear what the imposters had done with the information they solicited from Kiki and Etienne. The couple had not been to the bank or checked their accounts in the two weeks since the flooding had occurred. It wasn't until the police contacted them as part of a wider investigation that they were advised to check with their financial institutions and credit agencies.

"They informed us that these people were not Good Samaritans gathering our information for forwarding to FEMA. They had an ulterior motive, which was identity theft, or outright theft. Hence the form requesting bank details."

Afraid of what she might find out, Kiki couldn't bring herself to contact the bank. She and Etienne drove together to the nearest operational branch, and she waited in the car while he went inside.

"And then he came out and said everything was fine; the money was still there. We closed all our accounts and opened new ones, to be on the safe side. But I still felt very uneasy, because these people were out there with our information. And it seemed like it was just a matter of time before they used it for some criminal purpose. And then we got our credit reports and there it was."

The credit reports revealed page after page of new credit card accounts with hefty balances. The thieves had wasted no time in making use of the couple's good names and outstanding credit history.

Etienne describes his reaction. "We were infuriated. But we also felt violated, as if a predator had infiltrated our lives. We had lost so much already. It was a real blow."

I WAS JUST IN THE NEIGHBORHOOD

Floyd is a retired salesman. A widower, he lived on his own in the house where he and his wife had raised their family. One year, shortly after Halloween, he received a knock on the door. He opened it to find two men standing on his doorstep. They said they were passing and happened to notice that his chimney was crumbling. With winter coming on soon, they wondered if they could fix it for him. To leave it as it was would risk further damage and render the fireplace inoperable.

Floyd, who had not been up on the roof in 20 years, at first declined their offer. Then the younger of the two men, who introduced himself as Del, offered to go up there and take a closer look at no charge. Floyd reluctantly agreed. The men put a ladder up against the side of the house and disappeared. Shortly afterward, they reappeared at the door. They told Floyd that as they suspected, the chimney was falling apart and the loose bricks had already begun to cause some wear and tear on the roof shingles. Del showed Floyd a picture on his cell phone that he said he'd snapped on the roof. It did indeed show a crumbling chimney. Del advised Floyd to get the work done immediately.

Still Floyd wavered. He said that home improvements were his son's area, and his son wasn't due for a visit anytime soon. Del expressed concern. One big storm and the whole chimney could come down, leaving a gaping hole in the roof. Del said that if Floyd were his father, he'd want it done sooner rather than later. Pointing to his truck, he said that he and his cousin, Franco, could get started right away.

"I used to be a salesman," says Floyd. "He was giving me the hard sell, but that's his job. I used to go door to door myself. It's not that easy. He had the photographic evidence. So I asked him how much it would cost, and he quoted me a price that seemed fair. I told them to go ahead."

Roof repair would be the first of many jobs Del ended up doing for Floyd. As soon as one job ended, Del would find something else in or around the house that needed fixing. After a while, Floyd got used to having Del and his crew around.

"I live in Massachusetts and my son lives in Atlanta. He's a good kid, but he's busy with his job and his own family, so he doesn't make it up here too often. Del would come around and we'd have a chat. He saw the photos of my grandkids and he told me about his own young children."

Over a period of months, Floyd began to feel like Del was a member of his extended family. He asked after Del's family regularly, and Del seemed to enjoy listening to Floyd's stories about his past. It didn't matter to Floyd that there seemed to be no end to the number of projects Del was undertaking around the house. He convinced himself he was finally getting around to taking care of things that should have been done long ago.

"I'm not a handyman. Living alone, you don't get so fussy about what your house looks like and what works or doesn't. I wasn't surprised that there was a lot of stuff that needed doing. I just figured that I was doing it all at once instead of over the years, like most people do."

A lot of the work was supposedly taking place in areas that were inaccessible to Floyd, such as the roof, the gutters, and the attic. One day, Del checked out Floyd's basement and came back up with a plan to remodel the space.

"He said it looked like it hadn't been touched in 30 years, which was probably true. My son used to spend a lot of time in the basement when he lived at home, but after he left, my wife and I hardly ever went down there. And as I got older, it was harder for me to manage the stairs. They're pretty steep. Del talked about how, with some updating, it could be a great rec room for my grandchildren. He wanted to rip out the wood paneling, redo the floor, the whole works."

Del quoted Floyd a cost of $25,000 to renovate the basement. Floyd acquiesced. Around the time the basement work was scheduled to begin, Del told Floyd that his wife had been hospitalized after being struck in a hit-and-run accident. As a self-employed contractor, Del didn't have health insurance and was worried about being able to pay off the medical bills. Floyd offered to help out.

In his weekly phone call with his son, Allen, Floyd mentioned that he was having his basement renovated for the grandchildren. When Allen expressed surprise, his father said it was only one of many home improvement jobs he'd commissioned. Allen pressed him for more details on who was performing the services and how much he was paying for all of the work. At that point, Floyd began to feel a little defensive, as if his son was questioning his judgment. Allen made his father promise to hold off on having any more work done for the time being.

Although Floyd was annoyed at what he perceived as his son treating him like an untrustworthy child, he kept his promise and told Del that the basement renovation would have to wait a few weeks until his son's visit. The money for Del's wife's treatment, however, was a separate issue. Floyd wrote a check for $10,000.

Del continued to come around the house for the next couple of weeks, but he stopped abruptly when Allen arrived.

"My son went all around the house, looking at things Del was supposed to have fixed, and nothing had been done. He went up on the roof and said my chimney was fine. I told him it should be fine, because Del patched it up. He said, 'Dad, there's no way anyone's done any work on this roof recently.' Ditto the gutters, the insulation in the attic. Nothing that was supposed to have been done was done. Allen got my checkbook and statements and went through to see what had been paid out. That's when all hell broke loose."

Allen was horrified to discover that his father had paid Del more than $50,000 in less than six months. As he tried to explain to his father that he had been fleeced, he found Floyd disbelieving.

"I said there was just no way. I knew Del. He was a family man, a hard worker. He may have left some of the jobs unfinished because he knew he'd be coming back. There was no way he would cheat me. He showed up for work even with his wife in the hospital."

Allen asked his father to clarify the last point. That's when it emerged that Floyd had given Del money for hospital bills. To Allen, it was clear that his father had been taken, but to Floyd, there was a rationale for everything that had happened. He told Allen to wait and see. Del would be back and he would explain himself.

It was only when Del didn't reappear or return his messages that Floyd began to question the contractor's intentions. He consented to go to the police. Unfortunately, with no written contract and no contact information for Del other than his now-defunct cell phone, there was little the police could do.

Allen was incensed, but Floyd was more sad than angry. "I know it sounds strange to say this, but I missed having Del around. He had been good company. I enjoyed our conversations. That was a loss to me too."

Allen insisted that his father move out of the house and into a retirement complex. Del never resurfaced in Floyd's life.

Even in an era of advanced technology, some scam artists prefer to conduct their "business" the old-fashioned way—by knocking on your door. Door-to-door solicitations can be very effective in perpetrating scams. Once the front door is open, people can be intimidated, pressured, or charmed into revealing information or even handing over money.

There may be legitimate reasons for someone coming to your door. Perhaps the person represents a real company looking for your business. Maybe he or she is genuinely soliciting funds for a worthy charity or cause. But whether it's legitimate or not is irrelevant. In this and in all situations where cons can occur, the old adage holds true: prevention is better than a cure.

Contracting is a classic conduit for scams. Nearly 70 percent of American households own their homes. At some point, each one of those homes will require the services of a contractor such as a plumber, electrician, exterminator, or landscaper. For every service, there is a provider. Some are listed in the Yellow Pages, some advertise, and some rely on word of mouth. Others put a leaflet on your door or stop by because they were "just in the neighborhood" and noticed that the paint was peeling or that the driveway needed repaving. A common ploy is to say that they were working on another house in the neighborhood and can offer a discount because they have leftover materials.

Contracting scams are not complicated. They involve charging and in many cases overcharging for services that are not completed as promised. Real-life examples include companies hired for asbestos abatement who leave large traces of asbestos behind, chimney sweeps that tell customers their chimneys have holes in them and need costly repairs, and driveway repaving that costs thousands more than agreed and cracks within days. Many scamming contractors are transient, moving in and out of areas quickly in order to find new victims and to avoid being detected.

Senior citizens make especially easy targets. Many live alone. They may be more trusting and easier to manipulate. Because of physical limitations, they may not be in a position to verify that work needs to be or has been done. Once they have paid an unscrupulous contractor for work, they will be hit up again for more money. Scam artists have even been known to accompany elderly victims to the bank to access their money more quickly.

RUSE ENTRY BURGLARY

The FEMA imposters who targeted Kiki and Etienne never crossed the threshold, but plenty of door-to-door scammers do, under false pretenses. Louisa's mother, Hannah, had lived on her own for more than 15 years. One morning, as she was watering the plants, the doorbell rang. A man wearing an orange vest stood on her doorstep. He told her he was from the gas company. There had been reports of a gas leak in the area and he needed to come in and check her gas lines. When she hesitated, he warned her that if there was gas leaking, even something as simple as turning on a light could ignite the gas and cause an explosion. Any delay was dangerous.

"At that point, she didn't think she had a choice, so my mother let him in," Louisa explains. "Then a second man suddenly appeared. The first guy went into the kitchen with my mother; the other guy went in another direction. My mother started to get a little anxious having these two strange men in her house, but a couple minutes later, they said they were done and left."

When Hannah went into her bedroom, she found clothes strewn on the floor and drawers in the dresser pulled open. Her jewelry box was missing, as were several hundred-dollar bills Hannah kept in her nightstand. Among the jewelry stolen were pieces that had been in Hannah's family for generations, items that the family had brought with them from Russia when they immigrated in the 1920s.

"My mom didn't tell me for many days. I think she was afraid to tell me because she thought I would insist she move in with me, that it would prove she wasn't to be trusted on her own. But it was the opposite. I would never infringe on her independence like that. She was the one who started to become nervous about being alone. She worried that these guys would come back, or that other unscrupulous people would show up. We're talking about a woman in excellent health. She was a champion swimmer in her youth, always strong, always sharp as a tack. She couldn't stop blaming herself. The whole incident really took a toll on her confidence. That was hard to see." Hannah ended up moving in with her daughter voluntarily.

Ruse entry burglaries take place when the criminal impersonates someone—usually a utility or public service worker—in order to gain entry to a home. Once inside, the scammer and maybe an accomplice will steal cash, wallets, purses, checkbooks, or whatever other valuables they can find and can transport out of the house quickly.

Often, the perpetrators will be wearing or carrying something to make them look like the genuine article, whether it's the orange vest, a hard hat, or an ID dangling around the neck. It could be a fire department inspector who needs to see the smoke detectors. Maybe he's checking gas lines or testing the water. Whatever the reason for his visit, he'll need to come inside and look around. If working in pairs, one will distract the homeowner while the other commits the burglary.

If the homeowner is hesitant, as was the case with Hannah, they will up the ante. There's a possible gas leak or wiring problem that could lead to an explosion or fire. The water might be contaminated and unfit for drinking. If the occupant still refuses, there may be a threat to cut off service.

BUY, BUY, BUY

"I had a job one summer in college selling encyclopedias door to door," says Jun. "And in hindsight, it was probably some kind of scam too," he decides. "But I thought it was an honest job. I was always polite, never aggressive. What happened to my folks, I never could have imagined it."

Jun's parents, the Chongs, live in a predominantly Chinese neighborhood in New York. Their English is limited, but one day they opened their door to a young Chinese man who spoke to them in their native Mandarin.

"He told my mom he was new to the States and had landed this job selling a Chinese herbal remedy, kind of like vitamins. He made small talk with her, asked where in China they were from. He said he was from the same city, and they chatted about various landmarks there."

When the salesman complained of sore feet, Mrs. Chong invited him in for a glass of water. Her husband, who had been napping in the bedroom, woke to find his wife at the kitchen table with the young man.

"My dad was a little surprised, but pretty soon he was talking to the guy too. They both found him very engaging. And it's the Asian way to be very hospitable and courteous. After a while, he brought out a sample of the remedy he's selling, which boosts vitality, promotes long life, strengthens bones, eases aches and pains, all those good things. He gave his sales presentation. They listened politely. Then he got into pricing. My mom later told me that she thought it was going to be a matter of buying a bottle and sending him on his way, which she was willing to do. But he told them that it was something that you bought as a series. Every month, they would send you a new supply. The solution would be formulated according to the season, your age, specific ailments, etcetera. And because it was a daily dose, each month you would receive 30 individual doses. He was throwing figures at them like $1,800 for an annual supply."

The Chongs said they were not interested, but the salesman persisted, offering them a "hometown" discount of $300. Again, they declined. He went on, touting the benefits of the remedy, saying that it would add years to their life. He showed photos of his wife and baby in China, whom he hoped to bring over when he had raised enough money. He pleaded, saying that his cousin had hired him for this job and would be unhappy if he came back empty handed.

Jun was out of town at a conference when he received a call from his mother. "She said this man was in their house and wouldn't leave. I made her put him on the phone, and I spoke to him in Chinese. I asked him to leave my parents alone, to leave the house immediately. He was very apologetic and assured me he was on his way out. My conference session was just about to start, so I turned off the phone and assumed everything was resolved."

When Jun emerged from the session two hours later, there were two more messages from his mother, sounding increasingly distressed and asking him to call. When he returned the calls, he got a busy signal.

"I started to get worried, because I knew they had a stranger in their house. I tried calling a friend who lived in the area to see if she could go check on them. I thought about calling the police. Then I tried calling my parents again and finally got through."

Mrs. Chong told her son that even after being asked to leave, the salesman continued his pitch.

"He used every tactic in the book. My mother said she was very embarrassed because he started crying when he was talking about his family. She actually apologized to him and said they just didn't have the money to spend. Then apparently his mood turned. He accused them of not wanting to help their fellow countryman. He called them ungrateful, saying they had benefited from living in America but were unwilling to share the spoils."

After three hours of his haranguing and begging, the Chongs were tired and anxious and desperate to get the stranger out of their house. They finally agreed to pay him, using cash they kept in the house for emergencies.

Jun was furious. "As far as I'm concerned, he robbed my parents. He assaulted them, just not physically. He even managed to take the phone off the receiver so I couldn't reach them. He knew what he was doing. They're an older Asian couple; there's a good chance they'll have cash in the house. They'll be receptive to another Chinese person. He spoke to them respectfully at first, just like a son would to a parent."

The Chongs refused to go to the police, but they warned their friends and neighbors to be on the lookout. They never received the herbal supplement.

Door-to-door sales scams are plentiful. People will knock on doors offering to sell just about anything, including meat, artwork, candy, appliances, and carpets. Using high-pressure tactics and sometimes intimidation, they try to coerce people into buying something they don't want or need. When money has exchanged hands, the victims often never receive the promised goods. If they do receive their products, they usually find they have overpaid for substandard merchandise. Scammers will use whatever it takes to get the money. A woman in her 80s, nearly blind, paid door-to-door con artists for 200 years' worth of magazine subscriptions.

This is not to say that young, perfectly healthy people can't fall victim to the same swindle. It happens every day. Like the Chongs, many people, having already made the mistake of opening the door, pay the peddler just to get rid of him.

GIVING AT THE DOOR

Sometimes the doorbell rings and there's no orange vest, no sales, no leftover asphalt. There is just an outright request for money. But the money is for a good cause. It's for hungry children or for victims of that awful hurricane.

"What can I say? They seemed like a couple of sweet, fresh-faced kids." Vicki was home with her newborn when two young adults appeared on her doorstep. "It was a boy and a girl. The girl was super peppy and did most of the talking. She said they were part of the student orchestra at a local college and were trying to raise money for a summer tour of Europe. The fund-raiser involved having people buy toys and books that would be donated to a children's shelter. Was I interested in making a contribution? Well, it's hard to say no to that."

The "students" were well prepared. They had a pamphlet on the orchestra and shared details of their trip with Vicki. "I had done a tour of Europe when I was a student, so I was reminiscing about some of my favorite places. They seemed very excited about it. There was absolutely zero indication that anything was suspicious."

Johan, Vicki's neighbor across the street, found them agreeable as well. "I play the piano, so I asked them what instruments they played. I even asked for the names of their music professors, because a friend of mine teaches in the music department at the college."

Both Vicki and Johan made donations of $50. That weekend, Johan ran into his music professor friend. "I told him I'd given some money to support the student orchestra tour. He asked me what tour I was talking about. I told him it was the European tour. It was the first he'd heard of it. He said he'd double check, but he was pretty sure someone was pulling my leg. He got in touch with his department head, who is also in charge of the orchestra. There was no tour. But what about those students? I couldn't get my head around the fact that they weren't even students, just some budding con artists. They played their parts so well."

Johan and Vicki contacted the police, who confirmed that they had received several reports of the same scam. An investigation revealed that the phony student orchestra had taken thousands of dollars from well-meaning individuals all over town and throughout the county.

Vicki never imagined encountering crime in that form, particularly not in her neighborhood. "It's such a peaceful, nice place. Everyone's very friendly, it all feels very safe. Door-to-door con artists are just not what you expect to find around here."

There are a million legitimate needy causes in every neighborhood and around the world, but they generally don't come knocking on the door for funds. Door-to-door charity scammers can be creative in their storytelling and very convincing. To be successful, they need to be able to talk the talk. In another case, a man collected checks that he claimed would help military veterans and their families. The man, himself a veteran, then altered the payee name on the checks and cashed them.

The stories don't have to be convoluted. Sometimes the cons are straightforward and simple. A group of people went from house to house taking orders for sandwiches to benefit a local church. The sandwiches went for $5 a piece, but they never arrived. In the meantime, the church began receiving calls asking what the money would be used for.

Other times, the pleas are more personal. Farida had a house full of kids when she received a visitor. "It was a woman, probably about my age, late 30s. She looked stressed. She said she was new to the area and had locked her house keys, cell phone, and wallet inside her house. She asked me if she could borrow the phone to call a locksmith. Of course I let her in. The kids were very curious. I had to shoo them away to give her some privacy. But she was talking so loudly we couldn't help but overhear her. She said she needed to get back to work but didn't have enough gas to make it there. Then she told the locksmith she would have to meet him herself because her husband was in Iraq. And I could see her eyes were a little teary when she got off the phone. My heart went out to her."

Farida said she would have given the woman a ride if she hadn't had the kids with her. Instead, she offered her $40 for gas. The woman was very grateful and thanked her profusely. She told Farida her name was Mindy and gave her the name of the pizzeria in town where she worked. She promised to pay the money back as soon as she was able to get to her wallet.

When Farida's husband returned that evening, she shared the story of the damsel in distress. "He thought there was something weird about it, so he told me to call the pizza restaurant. I did, and sure enough, they said there was no Mindy employed there. Still, I thought it was some kind of mix-up. Then, a few days later, I saw the article about her in the local paper. Turns out she'd made the round of businesses and homes in the area. Same woman, same exact scenario. She's locked out, she needs money for gas, she makes a loud phone call, her husband's overseas."

Few decent people would turn down a request from someone in trouble. Scammers know this, and they use it to their advantage. If someone truly needs help, usually he or she doesn't go door to door looking for it. If someone knocks on the front door or shows up at the office with a hard-luck story, the intention is almost certainly to walk away with a little of your money. Fake sob stories often revolve around being stranded without transportation and communication. One man operating for years in the Washington, D.C., area tells a story about a broken-down car and needing to get to the hospital for a sick daughter. If you could just spare money for cab fare, it would really help him out. Sometimes he varies his story by saying that he needs to get to the funeral parlor to collect his dead son's body.

People who use this approach are invariably reported as being friendly, polite, even apologetic. They don't mean to put you out and hate to ask, but they're really in a jam. They're good actors and can cry on demand if they need to. If you feel there's any possibility someone is in real jeopardy or needs help urgently, offer to call the police. No con artist wants to involve the police, so if they refuse or start to waffle, it's time to move on.

PROTECTING YOURSELF

Put up a sign. It doesn't have to be fancy. "No solicitations. No handbills." This should weed out the vast majority of door-to-door solicitations and advertising. Check with your city or town to see what the regulations are regarding soliciting. Many municipalities prohibit soliciting at homes that display anti-solicitation notices. If you have put up a sign and still receive solicitations, you can file a complaint.

If you feel uneasy, don't answer the door. Hopefully a sign will deter door-to-door peddlers, but if it doesn't, simply don't answer the door unless you're expecting someone. If the person claims to be from a utility company, call the company to confirm. If you don't answer the door to a scammer, he or she will move on. Don't even give these people the time of day. If you heed this one piece of advice, you will not need to read any further. If, however, you make the mistake of opening your door and end up confronting a doorstep scam, make sure you follow all the steps below.

Don't hire someone who shows up at your door. If you need someone to work on your home, ask friends and family for recommendations. Check out the handiwork whenever possible. If you see a paint job you like in the neighborhood, find out who the painter was.

Don't pay any money up front. Contractors should not require you to pay anything up front. If they claim to need the money to buy supplies, this should be a warning sign. If it's a salesperson, well, why are you opening your door to salespeople? Don't open the door, don't buy anything, don't hand over any money. Period.

Get it in writing. Ask a contractor for a written quote. When you hire someone, make sure you have a signed contract that includes pricing, a clear description of the work to be completed, and a time frame.

Check with the authorities. Contact your state licensing board to find out if a contractor is licensed. Make sure they are insured before they begin work. You may also want to check with the state attorney's office to find out if anyone has filed a complaint against the company.

Don't rely on appearances. Identification is easy to forge. Vans are a dime a dozen. Anyone can put on a hard hat and work boots. Just because they look right doesn't mean they are. If someone claims to be from the utility company, call the company using a number you find yourself, not one provided by the person. Utility workers usually have appointments. They don't show up randomly asking to enter your home.

Give nothing away. Do not share personal information with people who come to your home unexpectedly and whose identities cannot be confirmed independently. For example, census takers represent the U.S. government, and people are legally obligated to talk to them; however, their identities can be verified by calling a regional census office.

Know your rights. The FTC's Cooling-Off Rule offers some protection for consumers who make a purchase in their home. Under the rule, you have three days to cancel purchases of $25 or more with a full refund. However, you must be notified about your cancellation rights at the time of purchase and the salesperson must provide two copies of a cancellation form and a copy of your contract or receipt. Other restrictions also apply. For more information, visit www.ftc.gov or call 1-877-FTC-HELP.

Give prudently. Charitable giving is a wonderful and generous act, but it should not be done at the door. The fact that an organization calls itself a charity and maintains a website does not mean it is legitimate. Check the Better Business Bureau's directory of accredited charities at www.bbb.org/us/charity/ to see if the charity in question is genuine.

Call the cops. If you feel threatened or intimidated in any way, call the police. If you have someone standing in your doorway, you're vulnerable. Don't put yourself in that position. Keep the phone handy. If you've told them to go away and they're loitering outside your home, call the police.

(6)

DIALING FOR DOLLARS

Fending Off Phone Fraud

Nancy's father and grandfather were decorated Navy veterans. Her husband, Phil, served in the first Gulf War. So when their younger son Jack enlisted in the Army shortly after graduating from high school, she was not entirely surprised.

"We were very proud of him. Then he got shipped off to Iraq and I was terrified. But still proud." Nancy became active in support groups for military families, collecting donations, shipping care packages, sewing quilts and blankets for expectant wives. It was a way for her to keep busy while spending time with other folks sharing the same deployment experiences.

When Jack returned to Iraq for a second tour, Nancy's anxiety grew. "He'd been lucky the first time, but how long was his luck going to hold out? The worry was always with me."

Late one night, the phone rang in Nancy and Phil's modest home in Lansing, Michigan. Caller ID showed an out of town area code and identified the call as coming from the Red Cross. Nancy and Phil exchanged glances. Neither wanted to answer the phone, but eventually Nancy did, fearing the worst.

"It was a woman. She asked for me by name, asked if I was Jack's mother. I said yes. My heart was pounding so hard I actually thought I might be having a heart attack. She was calling from the Red Cross. Jack had been hurt in a vehicle rollover. She didn't know the extent of his injuries, but it was serious enough that he had to be airlifted to Germany. His dog tags had been lost in the accident and he was unconscious. In order to complete the paperwork for his treatment, they needed his Social Security number and date of birth."

Panicked and distraught, Nancy began rifling through personal papers to find her son's Social Security number, which she rattled off to the caller.

"She was very calm and reassuring, said he was receiving the best care possible. They were going to update us on his condition within the hour." When the call was over, Nancy relayed the conversation to her husband and the two of them stayed up all night waiting for a follow-up call.

"As the hours passed by, I became certain he was dead. If everything was okay, why weren't they calling back right away?" Finally, shortly before sunrise, the phone rang again.

"It was the same lady. When she told me Jack was stable, I almost fainted. I was crying and laughing, thanking her. She said she was glad to be giving me good news." Then, almost apologetically, the caller asked Nancy if she'd care to make a donation to the Red Cross.

"Of course I did. How could I not? I gave her my credit card number for a $50 donation and asked her to put it in Jack's name."

Nancy felt overwhelming relief and gratitude. While Phil returned to bed, his wife buzzed with energy. She cleaned the house, quilted, and as soon as the hour was decent, began to call family members to pass on the news. Around midday, when the lack of a night's sleep was beginning to catch up with her, the phone rang yet again. This time it was Jack himself.

"I couldn't believe it. I started bombarding him with questions. Are you okay? What happened? Are you coming home? He could hardly get a word in edgewise. And all the time I was thinking, gosh, he sounds great for someone who's just been in an accident and airlifted. When I finally stopped to take a breath, he asked me what the heck I was talking about."

It took a moment for Nancy to understand what Jack was telling her. There had been no accident, no injury. The phone call she had received was phony. At first, she thought there must have been some mistake, that they'd called the wrong house, the wrong parent.

"Even after he'd told me he was fine, a part of me still thought the information was real. It's difficult to accept that someone would do such a thing. I kept telling him that she was from the Red Cross. Jack was the one who had to convince me that I'd been scammed. I'd handed over all his information and my credit card number to God knows who."

After getting off the phone with her irate son, Nancy phoned the Red Cross, and found out that if her son had been injured, the call would have come directly from the military, who wouldn't need to solicit any personal information. It was not the first time the Red Cross had heard of impersonators targeting military families.

"The woman who had called us was as helpful and kind as can be," said Nancy. "It never occurred to me that the call might not be genuine. Why would it? This person was a pro. She knew my name, knew Jack's name and where he was stationed. How would she get that kind of information? Who are these people?"

"These people" are individuals like Stella, a 40-something career hustler who has served time in prison for mail and wire fraud. Although not the person responsible for fleecing Nancy, she specializes in phone scams and has perpetrated several similar schemes. As Nancy's story is relayed to her, Stella nods repeatedly.

"The con is nothing without the story. If I call you and ask you straight up for money, it's like I might as well mug you in the street. There's no subtlety, no finesse. Deceiving someone requires effort. I have to somehow persuade you to give me what I want. To do that, I have to be convincing. And the more I know about you, the more convincing I can be."

At first, Nancy thought that someone she knew had been involved, because of the way she had been approached, and the references to her son's circumstances. Maybe it was an acquaintance of Jack's, or even someone from her own large social circle.

In general, Stella says, personal information is much more accessible than we think. "Military families in particular are pretty easy to spot. They love the flair. T-shirts, hats, stickers, posters, you name it. They advertise all over the place. They're sending packages and letters to their loved ones. They're openly communicating with each other online."

From the desk in her sewing room, Nancy can see the yellow ribbon tied around her mailbox, signifying the wait for Jack's safe return. On her lawn is a weather-beaten "Support the Troops" sign. In the driveway sits her Jeep Liberty. Its bumper sticker reads, "My Son is in the Army."

Nancy's morning routine includes surfing the Web. Her favorite sites are an online forum for mothers of deployed soldiers and a Facebook page for military families in her area. She estimates that she posts online four or five times a day, enough to be known as a regular. Her posts often mention Jack.

None of this is news to Stella. "Of course the Internet is a gold mine, but you'd be surprised at the amount of information someone can get from your car alone. Your daughter Courtney goes to Middlesex High School and plays trumpet in the band. You went to Texas A&M and are a donor. You belong to a union and vacation in the Outer Banks. I've also picked up useful tidbits just eavesdropping on conversations. A little bit of information can go a long way in establishing credibility. And of course, with the crisis call, there's an added element of urgency."

A crisis call has two built-in benefits for the con artist, presenting a situation that is both time sensitive and shocking. Victims must act quickly or further endanger a loved one. They are so upset that they don't think twice about giving out Social Security numbers, credit card details, whatever is requested. The natural inclination is to comply.

Looking back, Nancy wonders how she might have reacted differently. "When the caller said that Jack was injured, I could have challenged her, maybe, asked her why they would need that information, or just hung up and tried to call someone else. But it was the middle of the night. Who would I have called, and how long would that have taken? To be honest, when she told me he was hurt, my only thought was for my son, praying he wouldn't die, wishing I was with him. I would have done anything to help him. Anything."

Phone scams present a dilemma. Unlike a knock on the door, it's not always possible to avoid answering the phone. Genuine emergencies do arise. There are people you want and need to speak to on the phone.

In order for phone fraud to work, scammers need to keep you on the phone long enough to become interested and eventually committed to whatever con they're running. They will present some token that supposedly identifies them as a legitimate caller before asking you to recite a credit card number, wire money, share a Social Security number, or otherwise hand over valuable information or funds. The consequences of inaction are always presented as very negative. Your loved one will suffer, you'll be arrested, you'll miss out on millions, there will be no tax refund, and so on.

ALL IN THE FAMILY

Pete is a retired engineer. One day he picked up the phone to hear, "Grandpa, it's me."

Although he has two grandsons, one was only seven years old at the time. Assuming this was the older grandson, a college student, Pete replied, "Martin?"

The caller confirmed that he was Martin, and he sounded distressed. He told his grandfather he was in Vancouver, Canada, where he had been arrested for driving under the influence. He had five minutes to make one phone call.

"He said the police would let him go if he paid a fine and left the country. I had questions. Why didn't he call his folks? What was he doing in Canada?"

Martin claimed he had gone to Canada to visit a friend and was on his way back to the United States when he was pulled over. He pleaded for help, saying he was too ashamed to go to his parents. He'd pay back the money. Pete wavered. Sensing hesitation, Martin told him to expect a call from the U.S. consulate.

"Within minutes, I got a call from a man who said he was at the consulate in Vancouver. He backed up Martin's story, said it was a real headache for them, and could I get him out of there. I considered calling my son, Martin's dad, but then I thought, let's just get the kid home and deal with all the fallout later."

Pete withdrew $1,000 from his bank and went to a convenience store to wire the money.

"The consular official said I could expect a call from Martin when he got back to the U.S., so I waited for that. I didn't hear anything for the rest of the day, and I started to get worried that maybe the police hadn't received the money or they decided to keep him in jail. Finally I called my son Brian."

Brian, Martin's father, was shocked to hear the news. "He was a little angry I hadn't contacted him right away," said Pete, "but more concerned that we hadn't heard from Martin. Brian called his dorm room and there was no answer, left messages on his cell phone, even e-mailed him."

For several hours, there was no word from Martin. It wasn't until the next day that Pete heard from his grandson.

"Martin called me the next morning. He said he'd heard the whole story from his dad and didn't know what was going on. For a minute, I thought he was lying and trying to cover up. I asked why no one had been able to reach him. He said he'd been on a hike, out of cell phone range. I asked him about Canada. What about the arrest? He said he'd never been to Canada. He must have thought I was losing my mind."

Feeling like a patsy, Pete replayed the phone call over and over in his head, finally pinpointing the moment when he gave the imposter the upper hand.

"When I picked up the phone, he just said, 'Grandpa, it's me.' I'm the one who said, 'Martin?' I gave him the name. If I'd just asked who was calling, would he have known what to say?"

The tried and true grandparent scam relies on people's willingness to come to the aid of their grandchildren. They may be flattered that the grandchildren have chosen to call them instead of their parents. They feel good about being able to help. As seniors, they're likely to have savings accumulated. They're less familiar with their grandchildren's schedules and activities, so it's easier to fabricate a story about being in trouble. Pete rarely spoke to his grandson on the phone and never doubted that the voice was Martin's.

In a time of perceived crisis, it is difficult to take a step back and evaluate the situation. But it's imperative to wait. Con artists need you to act quickly, so don't give them the satisfaction. If someone calls with an emergency, do not do anything immediately. Instead, take steps to determine the authenticity of the call.

Do not take any caller's identity for granted. Probe for more details or ask an obscure question that only the real person could answer. Unexpected questioning can throw off a scammer and expose the scam. Think about what they are telling you. What doesn't make sense?

If it's an urgent call and someone is supposedly hurt or in trouble, independently verify that this is true. Call the person directly. Phone family members or friends to see if they know where the person is. Call the hospital where the person is supposed to be. Contact his or her employer.

OWE YOU? I DON'T EVEN KNOW YOU

There's no shortage of chutzpah where con artists are concerned. They are not confined to fabricating stories about a third person. In some cases, they try to talk people into believing a lie about themselves.

Karen, a registered nurse, began receiving phone calls out of the blue from a man calling himself Mr. Jackson. "The first time, he was polite. He said he was calling to collect on the money I owed him. My reaction was, what money? It was a very specific amount, $922.50. I told him I had no idea what he was talking about."

Mr. Jackson reminded Karen that she had applied for a loan online and that the amount had been transferred directly into her bank account. As proof, he recited her name, address, Social Security number, and e-mail address, information he said she had provided as part of her loan application.

"He seemed to know everything about me. He said if I didn't have the money readily available, I should borrow it from friends or family. He was going to call back in an hour to get my debit card number."

The call left Karen dumbfounded. "I thought it was a joke. But at the same time, it was very creepy."

As promised, Mr. Jackson called back in an hour, then twice more that day. In the week that followed, he called more than 50 times, leaving two dozen voicemail messages. Each one threatened legal action if he was not reimbursed.

"It got to the point where I wouldn't answer the phone. Every time he called, he said I'd better have the money or a good lawyer. He always ended with 'God bless you and your family,' as if that somehow made it less threatening."

In a debt collection con, the hope is that eventually the victim will be intimidated or tired enough to pay up. In this case, the phone calls were so persistent and harassing that Karen began to doubt herself. She wondered if while browsing on the Internet she'd somehow clicked on a link and applied for a loan unknowingly.

"There are so many of those pop-up windows. I thought maybe when I closed one of those, I'd accidentally gone through to a loan company or something. Even my husband asked me if I was sure I hadn't borrowed any money. The amount was weird; the guy was so sure of himself. And he wouldn't stop calling. I couldn't believe someone would go to so much trouble to try and get $900 out of me. I actually considered paying just to get him off my back."

Instead, Karen alerted the police, who tried calling the number Mr. Jackson had left. The voicemail box was full. The police traced the phone number to a cell phone registered under an alias, likely the name of an identity theft victim.

Phony debt collectors may use the name of an established company in an effort to sound more legitimate. They sometimes claim to be calling about a past-due utility bill that can be paid by credit card over the phone.

Karen found the experience surreal and frightening. "It was like being blackmailed, except that his grounds for blackmail were completely fictional. But the intimidation factor was very real."

ON OFFICIAL BUSINESS

Hank is a high school English teacher and self-described "straight arrow." One day, he returned home to find a voicemail from the county courthouse asking him to call as soon as possible. When he called the number left in the message, he was astounded to hear that a warrant had been issued for his arrest.

"The clerk said that I had failed to turn up for jury duty. The irony is, I had always wanted to be picked for a jury. I thought it would be an interesting experience. But as I said to the woman, I never received a jury summons."

Hank was mortified at the thought of being in trouble with the law. Luckily for him, the court clerk was sympathetic. "She sort of sighed and said this kind of thing happens all the time, that it was probably never sent out or lost in the mail. They could make the warrant go away, but I would still need to pay a fine."

The court had Hank's name and address, but to verify his identity, he had to provide a Social Security number. Then she took his credit card number for the fine. Hank didn't give the episode another thought until a couple of months later, when he tried to trade in his car for a newer model.

"I was sitting with the financing person in the dealership and he ran a credit check for the car loan. There was a problem with my credit. He couldn't approve the loan. I couldn't believe it. I'd never had a problem getting credit before. He advised me to get a copy of my credit report, which I did."

More surprises awaited Hank. His credit report showed that two new credit card accounts had been opened in his name, with an accumulated outstanding debt of $22,000. Shortly afterward, Hank, who had never received so much as a parking ticket, began receiving calls from collection agencies.

"I was aware of identity theft. I knew it existed. I'm not naive. But to target me in this way, so deliberately, the whole jury story, engaging me in conversation, I didn't expect that. It was more like a scene you'd see in a movie, not something that would happen in real life. It took me months to get my credit straightened out, and they still have my Social Security number, so I always have to be vigilant."

The scam that hit Hank exists in different forms, but it always involves someone calling on official government business who requires personal identifying information or payment, or both. Like all swindlers, the callers are practiced and persuasive. Official business has the ring of authority. Unless you're an attorney (and even then), you may not be familiar with the law or your rights. And you don't want to get on the wrong side of Uncle Sam, so you may comply first and ask questions later. They're counting on it.

For just about every government agency, there is an accompanying scam. Seniors hear from callers offering discount prescription plans or replacement Medicare cards. Taxpayers receive calls from phony IRS representatives promising tax refunds. Voters are asked to confirm their voter registration and eligibility by providing Social Security numbers. Students applying for federal financial aid are another popular target, since they have dealings with the government and are known to be seeking funding. Companies charge them exorbitant fees for information that is freely available, such as scholarship listings, or falsely guarantee that they will find them aid.

In Michigan, con artists phoned unemployed workers claiming to represent Michigan Works, a job placement agency affiliated with the state's Department of Labor. The jobseekers were told that in order to be considered for current openings, they would need to provide Social Security numbers, birth dates, and bank and credit card account numbers. Those who did had their money and identities stolen, leaving them even worse off.

WHEN THE MESSAGE IS MISLEADING

Combining the authoritative air of the official business scam with the urgency of the crisis call is the phony alert, in which crooks use legitimate financial institutions as a front for soliciting private information.

Donna was driving home from work when she received a text message on her cell phone. It was her credit union, saying that her bank card had been deactivated. The message instructed her to call a toll-free number, where she was prompted to enter her debit card and PIN numbers.

"I was annoyed, because this wasn't the first time the credit union had screwed up something on my account. So I put in the numbers and then the line just went dead. That's when I started to get a really bad feeling. I couldn't call the credit union to check because it was after hours and they were closed."

Sitting in rush-hour traffic, with an increasing sense of dread, Donna made a quick decision. "If the whole thing was a hoax, I could think of only one thing to do. I didn't know what these people were planning to do, but obviously whatever information I'd given them was enough to get into my account."

Donna immediately drove across town to the nearest credit union branch. Using her now compromised debit card, she withdrew the maximum daily limit, $500.

"I went home with my money and told my boyfriend what had happened. He asked me why I didn't take out more money, and I told him there was a limit on withdrawals. Then it occurred to us that if it was a daily limit, we could withdraw another $500 as soon as the new day began. So we stayed up way past our bedtime and drove over to the ATM just before midnight. Right at midnight, I was in there taking out another $500. That left about $20 in the account, which I guess could have paid for a couple of pizzas but not much more."

Donna's quick thinking saved her. When she went into the credit union the next day to change her account information, she was told that the text scam had already hit hundreds of the bank's customers, many of whom had not been as lucky as Donna.

Phony alerts are confusing because the setup for the scam is to tell you that you've been the victim of a scam. Your believing that it is true is what makes the scam successful. Adding to the confusion is the fact that calls alerting you to security breaches on your account do also come from legitimate sources. We rely on our financial institutions to let us know if they've detected suspicious activity on our accounts. However, a real financial institution will not call and ask you for account numbers and other private information. If you receive a call of this nature, end the call without divulging any personal details. Then take your card out from your wallet and call the toll-free number on the back. If the alert was legitimate, they'll be able to help you out from there.

TELEMARKETING TRICKS

David looked like a man who had it all. A recent law school graduate, he had landed a well-paying job as an associate in a respected firm. He and his fiancée bought a house and were busy planning their life together. But even with his substantial salary, David carried large balances on multiple credit cards, a holdover from his student days. Six-figure student loans, a mortgage, and the upcoming wedding added to his financial burden. Still, when he received an automated message offering to help lower the interest rate on his credit cards, he deleted it. Then he and his fiancée went to look at venues for the wedding.

"We live in a big city. There are lots of options for wedding receptions, but none of them are cheap, at least none that she was interested in. Then you've got catering, flowers, cake, photographer, you name it. I had no idea. Our parents were not in a position to help much. Nor did I want them to."

When David returned home, he had a second, identical voicemail message promising lower credit card rates. "Just out of curiosity, I called the number and got connected to a customer service representative. She said her company could act on my behalf to negotiate lower interest rates for all my credit cards for a flat fee of $500. I told her I'd think about it. She referred me to their website for more information."

The website looked genuine, with cheery endorsements from satisfied customers. It all appeared and sounded professional. "The fee was high, but she said in some cases, they could cut the rates in half, not just reduce them by a point or two. After I looked at the site, I did the math, and there was the potential for me to save thousands of dollars. That's a honeymoon's worth of savings."

After paying the $500, David heard nothing. "They had told me it would take approximately a week, but that they would notify me as soon as the new rates were in effect. I was excited to find out how much I would be saving. But there was no communication. I called to check and they kept stalling, saying it was in the works. I e-mailed and received no response. I must have called 20 times. The final time, it just rang and rang."

Concerned, David contacted his credit card companies and discovered that no contact had been made on his behalf. If he was interested in negotiating interest rate reductions, he could do it himself at any time for no charge, but rates would only go down a point or two at the most. The next day, he received his bank statement. More bad news. The check he had written for $500 to cover the service had been altered to read $1,500. Instead of saving money, he was even deeper in debt.

Telemarketing calls such as the one David received are the original phone scams. Telemarketers have been around almost as long as the telephone, interrupting dinner with an offer on carpet cleaning or to ask for a donation in support of firefighters. Although not always a con, they are very rarely welcome.

Since the creation of the National Do Not Call Registry (see "Protecting Yourself"), calls from legitimate businesses have tapered off, making it easier to identify the shady calls, which are most of them. Examples of telemarketing fraud are bogus calls on behalf of real charities, medical insurance or prescription discounts, investment opportunities, mortgage relief, and employment assistance. As with all scams, the intent is to get an individual to provide something for nothing or to acquire information that will allow them to steal your identity and run up debts in your name. Automated or "robo" calls are used increasingly to reach a large number of people at once.

The federal government's crackdown on a notorious car warranty robocall campaign shows how widespread these efforts can be. The calls were so pernicious that a federal court issued restraining orders against the responsible parties, while the Federal Trade Commission filed suit against the two companies involved. The companies were found to be generating as many as one billion automated calls. The calls, made to nearly every phone number in the United States, claimed that the recipients' car warranties were expiring. Some people were tricked into thinking that the calls came from car manufacturers or dealerships. Those who bought the warranties found that they had overpaid considerably for very limited or nonexistent coverage.

BOILER ROOM BUNKUM

One specialized form of telemarketing involves the sale of something far more grand than car warranties. In the case of boiler room scams, callers are selling a piece of the American dream—the chance to strike it rich.

Jess and Arvin are a solidly middle-class couple with two kids. Arvin works in upper management at a nationwide retailer; Jess is a university administrator. By mutual agreement, Jess handles household finances and Arvin the couple's combined investments.

One day, Arvin took a call from a financial advisor named Sam. Before Arvin was able to hang up on him, Sam said, "I'm not selling anything. I just have something to tell you." Sam gave Arvin the name of a publicly traded company and said that its stock price would rise the next day.

"I was intrigued enough to check," said Arvin. "The next day, that particular stock had gone up."

Sam called back. He still didn't want anything, but he gave Arvin the name of a second company. That company's stock also rose. By the third day, Arvin was more receptive to Sam's calls.

"Imagine if you had money invested in those companies," Sam told him. "You'd be a happy man."

As Arvin remembered it, "He said he knew of another stock that was also guaranteed to rise. It was a pharmaceutical company and they were about to announce a breakthrough on Alzheimer's disease, but I had to act quickly if I wanted to get in on the action. The shares were still below market value but were about to explode, based on this forthcoming announcement. He told me the company's name. I looked it up. It was a legitimate company, listed on NASDAQ."

Arvin asked a lot of questions, but Sam had an answer for everything. Arvin wanted to know why the share price hadn't gone up already if the breakthrough was common knowledge. It wasn't common knowledge, but Sam had been following the company's research closely. Arvin asked why he was calling out of the blue. Sam said his background was in pharmaceutical sales and every once in a while he liked to challenge himself by making some cold calls. It helped to keep the job interesting. And it wasn't entirely random; Sam was working from a list of people who met certain age, income, and geographic criteria.

"Sam kept emphasizing the importance of timing. If I wrote a check on the spot and sent it to him overnight, he could make sure the money was invested by lunchtime. How much did I want to put in? At this point I hadn't agreed to invest a dime and I wasn't sure I wanted to."

Sam referred back to the first two tips he had given Arvin, saying if he chose to do nothing, he could sit back and watch while this new stock made millionaires of other people. Or he could be one of them.

"He was assertive, but all salespeople are. And although there was something appealing about it, I was hesitant, which is when he asked me if I had a 401(k). I said yes. He said, 'How's that working out for you?' That hit home, because Jess and I had both experienced big losses over the previous year. Sam's investment didn't seem any more risky. In fact, it seemed like it had the potential to be a lot more lucrative. He said it was a guaranteed investment. I don't believe any investment is guaranteed, but I did believe that it had a much better than average chance of succeeding, with better returns. And if the price went down, for whatever reason, I'd wait it out, just like with my 401(k)."

Arvin didn't have much spare money to invest, but he sent off a check for $5,000. He decided not to tell his wife, hoping to surprise her when the investment really took off.

"Sam called the next day to say he'd received my check and then again the next day to tell me the money had been invested and the paperwork was on its way. He told me to keep an eye on the price, that a big announcement was scheduled for the following week. I became a little obsessed. I started checking the share price several times a day, refreshing my computer screen."

Several days later, the paperwork from Sam still hadn't arrived, but Arvin didn't become concerned until the company's share price, which had been creeping up, suddenly plummeted. He called the office number Sam had given him, but there was no reply.

"I thought I'd copied down the wrong number. I decided to call the pharmaceutical company directly, to see if I could somehow trace him through the stock purchase. The company was real. They even did Alzheimer's research. But they had no record of my being a shareholder."

Arvin had been taken in by a classic boiler room scam. Mike, a veteran boiler room operator, now advises law enforcement agencies. As he describes it, the setup is typically run out of a crowded room of telemarketers.

"A lot of them are young and hungry, but there are a few old timers in the mix too. The old timers tend to make the big bucks. The job is pretty straightforward. Talk it up, get the money."

In a boiler room scenario, callers are "selling" worthless or fraudulent investments to unsuspecting members of the public. The scams work in various ways.

Mike's specialty was foreign currency trading. "Our shop worked on a script. You start off by saying a little something about how currencies are constantly fluctuating and how even a tiny fluctuation can lead to a huge profit. All we had to do was make it sound good. We tell them, the way we work it, you make money no matter what happens in the market. I would ask them to go get a pen and paper so we could run the numbers. Psychologically this is important, because you've now got them following your instructions. So they get the paper and you give them a bunch of numbers. If the dollar goes up, you make money here. If the yen goes down, you make money over here. It's a win-win. Did it make sense? Probably not. But currency trading is complex. People don't necessarily expect to understand it. They do understand what it means to make a grand a week, which is what we were promising."

What about the hot stock tips that are used to lure in people like Arvin? According to Mike, it's the luck of the draw. "Let's say I choose 20 companies at random. Then I call 20 people and give them each a stock to watch. The next day, I check the paper. If the stock I gave you went up, I call immediately and say, 'See, what did I tell you?' I do that two, three times in a row and you start to think I'm someone worth listening to. If the stock goes down, I don't call. It's easy and effective."

Common to boiler room schemes is the idea that investors are being let in on something hush-hush, that there is a new product or technology on the horizon that will send the investment's worth sky high, making the investor an overnight millionaire. Callers may drop the name of a celebrity or major financial institution that is poised to invest. The victim is made to feel part of an elite group.

As with all scams, time is of the essence. "Once they were hooked, we needed to have the money in hand as quickly as possible to avoid detection," Mike says. "We didn't want them to get cold feet or go to the authorities. All the callers were trained to suggest wiring money or using an overnight service to send a check or money order. Sometimes people would give a credit card number over the phone."

MAKE THE RIGHT CALL

The telephone is a convenient tool for swindlers, who are no longer confined to landlines. Scam calls can be live or automated. There are no visual clues to arouse your suspicion. A phone call is immediate and personal. A con artist can spin you a story quickly and convincingly. You're on the spot. And if they don't get the desired response the first time, they can call back again and again. Caller ID is not always helpful, since technology allows for the disguising of phone numbers, making a call from halfway around the world appear as if it's coming from your neighborhood.

To add insult to injury, people who have been victimized once can be burned again, in a process known as "reloading." Reloaders contact victims of fraud, claiming to be from a government agency or consumer organization and offer to help them regain their lost money. Of course, this help does not come free, but it's not until they've paid up that the targets realize they've been double scammed. Reloading also works by offering some incentive to the victim to continue paying, a kind of "double or nothing" deal. The individual is told that by parting with an additional sum of money, they will recoup their original loss and gain a bonus on top of that. Depending on the original scam, this can be a sum of money or prize merchandise of some sort.

Cutting off callers feels impolite and abrupt. It goes against all the rules of etiquette instilled in us as children. But if you find yourself on the receiving end of what feels like a dishonest call, there is absolutely nothing wrong with saying, "No, thanks." It may take a few tries, but be firm. If you are not sure about the authenticity of the call and it's an urgent matter, simply end the conversation as quickly as possible and find other means of verifying the information. Skepticism can be a powerful form of self-defense. Exercise it often.

PROTECTING YOURSELF

Join the Do Not Call Registry. Add your telephone numbers to the National Do Not Call Registry by phone at 1-888-382-1222 or online at www.donotcall.gov. Remember to register both your landline and your cell phone numbers. Registration is free. If your number is in the registry, it is illegal for telemarketers to call you.

Do not disclose any confidential information. If someone calls claiming to be from your financial institution, tell them you will need to call them back. Hang up. Then call the institution using a number that you know is legitimate (e.g., from your account statement or ATM card).

Don't wire money. Wiring money is as good (or bad) as sending cash. There's no way to get it back.

Keep quiet. Do not engage in conversation with cold callers. Consider all incoming calls suspect until you have confirmed the identity of the caller. There is no need to ever provide any personal information over the telephone to a stranger during an unsolicited phone call.

Do not donate to charities over the telephone. Legitimate charities have numerous ways of receiving donations. There is no reason to donate over the telephone and many reasons not to.

Report harassing phone calls. If the same people are calling you repeatedly, contact your phone company to find out what their policy is regarding harassing phone calls. If the calls are threatening, contact your local police department.

Do not call back using a number the caller has provided. Do not be fooled by caller ID. Scammers have the software to alter their phone number so it appears that they are calling from a familiar or local number even when they are calling from overseas.

Never invest in a stock or fund pitched over the phone. Enough said.

Contact the authorities. As always, if you feel you've been targeted by a scam, even if you haven't paid out any money, contact the police department. This can help them warn other potential victims.

(7)

FORTIFYING THE FIREWALL

Evading Electronic Scams

"It's a good living," says Darius, "and it's not that hard." A 25-year-old college dropout, Darius makes six figures a year. He works from home, has flexible hours, and is self-employed. When asked to describe his job, he usually says he's a computer programmer. "Sometimes I say I'm in sales, which is probably more accurate. I work with computers, but I'm the first to admit that I'm no tech geek."

In reality, Darius is one of a growing breed of computer scammers whose knowledge of computers is just enough to make them very dangerous. An enterprising criminal, Darius discovered that a small investment on his part could reap great rewards.

"It's like taking candy from a baby. I don't even have to write the code myself. I just go online and buy it."

"It" is a *crimeware* kit, a form of software intended for use in the commission of cybercrimes. Just as other people might buy the newest version of Microsoft Office, Darius purchased the latest version of a popular crimeware kit. Once installed on his computer, it allowed him to target unsuspecting computer users in order to infiltrate their systems. Once inside, he can gain access to personal data that enables him to tap into their bank accounts, follow their online movements, and retrieve credit card numbers and other financial information.

"Credit card numbers, bank account details, Social Security numbers, names, addresses, birthdates, passwords, PIN numbers—once you get on someone's computer and start monitoring their activity, it's amazing the amount of information you can get your hands on."

Alisha is close in age to Darius. A recent college graduate, she works full-time in a physician's office and earns $25,000 a year.

"I'm a phlebotomist," she says, "which means I collect blood samples. No one's all that thrilled about having their blood drawn, but I'm good at it, so it's quick and painless."

Alisha, like most of her generation, grew up using computers. She admits to being a cell phone addict and has a laptop computer. She uses the Internet to shop, pay bills, make travel arrangements, call friends, check the weather forecast, and much more. Alisha considers herself a responsible computer user. She updates her anti-virus program regularly and installs software updates when alerted.

"One evening I was meeting a friend for dinner. I like to look at restaurant menus beforehand, just out of curiosity and also to save time. I went online and searched for the restaurant by name. Sure enough, they had a website, but when I clicked on the link, a warning message popped up to say that the site could infect my computer."

The message instructed Alisha to click on a button to return safely to her search engine. She complied. Unbeknownst to her, by clicking on the button, she had installed a program that would begin to log all her keystrokes, giving a cybercriminal remote access to everything she typed into her computer, from personal e-mail messages to logins and passwords.

When a victim like Alisha installs a malicious program, Darius receives notification that the program has been activated. All he has to do then is to wait for the information to come flooding in. At first, Darius used the information he obtained to lift money from people's accounts and to make charges on their credit cards. Once he realized there was a huge underground market for stolen personal information, he became a supplier. With his crimeware running 24-7, Darius sits back and lets his computer do most of the work. The data stream in continuously, and every hour brings in new victims.

"I just gather the information and pass it on," Darius says. "It's easier to be the middle man." His customers then use the personal information to perpetrate identity theft and other forms of fraud.

After clicking on the pop-up message, Alisha continued using the computer as she normally would. Meanwhile, the keystroke program was shadowing her every move, as she logged into her bank account, accessed her credit card account, signed into Facebook, and checked her e-mail. She noticed that her computer was moving a little slower than usual but put it down to the age of the laptop.

Alisha didn't notice anything amiss with her accounts until two weeks later, the end of the month, when she went online to schedule her bill payments.

"I logged onto my bank's site and my accounts came up as usual, except that the balances were all off. I had an overdraft of $1,600 in my checking account and my savings account was completely empty. My paycheck goes in by direct deposit, and I knew that had just gone in the day before, so there is no way it could have been in deficit. And anyway, I always try to keep a balance of at least $200 in my checking account. My savings account should have had more than $2,000 in it. Some of that was money I'd received when I graduated from college. I was saving up to buy a car."

Her first thought was that it was a computer glitch, so she called the bank's customer service number. "They told me I'd authorized the transfer. I said it wasn't me. Then they said that whoever had done it used my user name and password to get in. It made no sense to me, because I had never shared that information with anyone. I never even wrote it down anywhere. It was all in my head. Then the woman asked me if anyone else had access to my computer. Again, no. But that got me thinking."

Alisha shared her story with a friend whose field was information technology (IT). He offered to come over and take a look at her computer. "He's the one who mentioned that it's possible for people to install these programs on your computer remotely. He asked me to go back and think about anything out of the ordinary I'd done online, if I'd received any unusual messages or anything. That's when I remembered about the restaurant's site and the warning message."

Alisha's friend was able to remove the malicious software from her computer, but she had no way of knowing to what extent her personal information had been compromised. "I had to assume they had access to everything, so I had to close every account, change all my cards and numbers and logins. I even considered getting a new Social Security number, but that seemed like it might be more hassle than keeping my old number. But I couldn't change my name or my address, my birthday. Someone could be masquerading as me this very minute. And it's my never-ending job to keep on top of it. Plus whoever it was could see all my personal messages. It's like having a stalker inside your head."

The Internet and e-mail have revolutionized our lives, making it possible to communicate at lightning speed, conduct personal and business affairs anytime anywhere, keep up with the latest news, and track down long-lost friends. Unfortunately, technology has also been kind to criminals, opening up a whole new frontier that they've been quick to exploit. Although they take advantage of the latest technology, e-mail and Web-based cons are in actuality no different from any other scams. They generally fall into one of the following categories:

- *Identity theft*—someone appropriates personal information, such as a credit card or Social Security number, to commit fraud or other crimes. Alisha's case fell into this category when someone emptied her bank accounts using confidential information extracted from her computer.
- *Advance fee fraud*—the payment of a fee or fees up front in return for a reward or merchandise that never materializes. This type of fraud often includes the use of the con artist's favorite device, fraudulent checks, which give the transactions the appearance of legitimacy and help persuade victims to comply.
- *Overpayment scams*—someone posing as a buyer overpays for an item or items by check and requests that the extra funds be wired back to them or sent to a third party who will take care of shipping. By the time the check is discovered to be a fraud, the seller has lost the amount of the wire transfer.

WITH FRIENDS LIKE THAT

Christian has 257 Facebook friends, including Gina, a former co-worker. While logged into his account one day, an instant message from Gina popped up on his screen. He began the chat by asking how she was. "Not great," she replied. She and her husband were on vacation in Paris and had been robbed. "Got money wired, but still short $200," the message said. "Can u help?" At first, Christian was sympathetic. "So sorry . . . that's terrible," he wrote. Then he started to wonder. "Is this really you? What's your husband's name?" "Shaun," the chatter replied correctly. "Of course it's me." Still not convinced, Christian asked, "How do we know each other?" The answer was quick. "School." Christian immediately deleted Gina from his list of friends and blocked her from contacting him again.

"I tracked down Gina by phone because I thought she ought to know that somebody had somehow gotten into her account and was posing as her."

Gina picks up the story. "He wasn't the first. I'd already had four or five friends call or text or e-mail to see if I was all right or what was happening. Christian was the only one who'd seen through it immediately. Others found it weird but thought I might really be in trouble. One, my cousin, went ahead and wired $100. And those are just the people who told me they'd been contacted. I'm sure they went through my whole list of friends, which is hundreds of people."

In trying to trace the source of the account hijacking, Gina remembered a notification she had received via e-mail shortly before it happened. "It looked like any other notification, saying that one of my friends had posted something on my wall. The note said, 'Remember this?' I was curious, so I clicked on the link in the message. It took me to the Facebook site and asked for my login and password, so I entered them. But when I got to my page, I couldn't see any sign of the 'Remember this?' message. I thought maybe my friend had sent it out, then changed her mind and deleted it."

The message Gina received was a fake, identical to a real Facebook notification, except that its purpose was to capture her account login information in order to bombard her friends with requests for money. Gina managed to resolve the situation by contacting Facebook directly and resetting her password. She then sent out an apology to all the friends on her list. "Scamming me was one thing, but then they scammed my friends. I felt like it was my fault. I still don't know how many people fell for it. I think there were others who gave money but didn't want to admit it. I learned my lesson. I never click on links in e-mails anymore.

If I get a notification, I go to the site first, log in, and check that way. I'm still really wary of it. I sometimes wonder if some of the people I'm linked to are even who they say they are. How would I know?"

Through Facebook, Twitter, MySpace, LinkedIn, and hundreds of other sites, you can now expand and keep up with your virtual entourage through a helpful selection of online tools. Special interest sites allow users to congregate in cyberspace with those who share similar interests in music, religion, politics, sports, and much more. They provide a forum for professional exchanges and linkages for academics, businesspeople, artists, and others. The problem with these outlets is that in cyberspace, identity verification is problematic. This makes the Internet a treasure trove for con artists. It provides camouflage, speed, and access to millions.

There are several ways to scam people through social networks. Hijacking accounts like Gina's is a popular ploy. Other cons have also migrated to social networking sites, and con artists don't need to be hackers in order to reach victims. Many people allow their information to be accessible, if not to the general public, then to a smaller, but significantly large number of people—for example, people who work for a certain company or live in a particular city. Remember, conners are always looking for ways into people's pockets. If you have listed modeling as an interest and you are suddenly approached by a modeling agency offering to put together a portfolio for you, it's not a coincidence.

THE BULL MARKET

Classified ads are a useful device for con artists. Online classifieds are free, instantaneous, and at your fingertips. But in the online marketplace, buyers are not the only ones who need to beware.

Tad and Nari own a two-bedroom apartment in Chicago. Tad was transferred to his company's office in Canada for a yearlong assignment. "We were newlyweds, and rather than fly back and forth all year, we decided to rent out our apartment in Chicago and move to Vancouver together for the year," says Nari.

They listed the apartment in an online ad and received a response right away. "It was from a man in Rio de Janeiro, a college professor. He was going to be a visiting lecturer at DePaul University and needed a place to live. Great. Sounded perfect. He asked all sorts of questions about the neighborhood, public transportation, how far it was from the campus. He seemed very enthusiastic and excited about coming to the States."

The couple asked for a month's deposit and the first month's rent up front, which came to $3,200. Meanwhile, they found a place in Vancouver and rented a unit to store their personal things while they were gone.

The renter, Professor Gomes, said that his employer, a university in Brazil, would be paying for his rent. Tad and Nari were told to expect a check in the mail. When the check arrived, they were in for a surprise. "It was for $15,000, way more than the rental amount. We contacted Professor Gomes and told him what had happened. He was laidback about it. He said the check had come directly from the university and they'd mistakenly sent a check to cover all his moving expenses, including airfare, shipping, and whatever else. We needed our share of the money, but he also needed money to buy his plane tickets and pay for his move."

The would-be tenant told Tad to deposit the check, deduct the rent money owed, and return the balance to him via wire. "I went ahead and did it," says Tad. "I'd heard that wiring money could be risky, but in my mind, that applied to wiring your own money, and as far as I was concerned, I wasn't wiring my own money. I was sending his money back to him."

After wiring the money, Nari and Tad proceeded to pack up their apartment and prepare for their move to Canada. They e-mailed the professor to tell him the money had gone through. He replied to thank them and said that he was looking forward to his trip to Chicago. That was the last time they heard from him.

"Tad wired the money on a Monday. On Thursday, I tried to pay for something at the store with our ATM card and it was rejected. When I called the bank, they said there were insufficient funds. It made no sense, because we had a decent balance, and besides, Tad had just deposited the rent money. I asked about the check we just deposited. Apparently, the issuing bank had rejected it. I couldn't quite believe it, so I kept asking for someone more senior to talk with. But they all said the same thing. The money had never been in our account because there was no money. But the money that Tad wired, that was real money—our money, which we now owed the bank."

Tad and Nari tried to contact their mystery tenant with no success. When they attempted to find someone by the name of Gomes at a university in Rio, they quickly realized that not only was that unlikely to be his real name, but they had no way of knowing if he was or ever had been in Brazil.

Online ads are a handy way to perpetrate an overpayment scam. Farmers in Missouri used the state's Department of Agriculture website to advertise and sell hay and found themselves cheated by thieves claiming to be buyers. The sellers received phony checks for more than the cost of the hay and were asked to refund the balance via wire transfer. The original checks were bogus, and the farmers were out thousands of dollars.

Raymond, a federal law enforcement officer, has seen his share of classified scams and points out that scammers also pose as sellers.

"The strangest story I ever heard was about a house for rent in Miami. The family that owned it—let's call them the Smiths—was moving to Ohio, but they wanted to hold onto the house because they planned on moving back to Florida eventually, and it was in a prime location. They listed it online through their local newspaper's website. Meanwhile, over in New Mexico, there was another family, the Johnsons, moving to Miami. They were looking for a house to rent and they went online to browse the listings. They came across this house. There were photos, it looked great, the rent was within their budget. Fantastic. So the Johnsons contact the landlords. The only problem is that the people they contacted were not the real landlords. They were crooks who saw the original ad and lifted it, photos and everything, and reposted it on a different site. Now the crooks were posing as the owners."

The scammers told the Johnsons the house was theirs to rent. The Johnsons sent the rent money to a post office box in Miami. "Usually the scam would stop there, with the payment. But in this case, the con men sent the Johnsons a fake lease. They also told them the keys had been misplaced, so they should go ahead and have the locks changed when they arrived."

The Smiths, still living in their Miami house, were awoken early one day by the sound of drilling. Mr. Smith looked out the window and saw a moving truck at the curb. Puzzled, he asked his wife if the moving company had somehow mixed up the days. She asked what the noise was all about. Making their way downstairs, they found a locksmith drilling a hole in their front door.

"It was the Johnson family, ready to move in. They were changing the locks, just as instructed. And they had papers to show the locksmith that they were entitled to change the locks. Of course the papers were phony, the Smiths were still in residence, and the whole thing was a sham. I always thought the con men were probably watching the whole thing, laughing. It's as though they purposely added insult to injury by getting that poor family all the way to the front door. The Johnsons were out of pocket a couple thousand dollars in rent money, they had nowhere to live, and they had a truckload of possessions to unload."

Similar schemes flourish on online auctions, which should be negotiated with care. Sellers may misrepresent merchandise or offer to sell merchandise that they do not have. Buyers may attempt overpayment with false checks. In addition to wire services, any suggestion of using an online escrow service or paying by cashier's check are red flags. Escrow services are supposed to accept your payment and then forward it on to the seller once your goods have been received. However, many online escrow sites are phony, set up by the scammers to receive your payments directly.

LOST AND FOUND

Animal lovers Amy and Steve adopted their black Labrador retriever, Addie, from a rescue organization when she was six. They doted on her, letting her sleep on their bed at night despite her size.

"She thought she was a lap dog," says Amy. "She was kind of nutty, but full of love. We called her Love Dog."

As she got older, Addie became prone to wandering off. "Our backyard wasn't fenced in, and she'd often scramble through the bushes and explore other people's yards. We tried to keep an eye on her, but we weren't very vigilant about it, especially after the birth of our baby. Sometimes we'd stand at the back door and yell out her name for 5 or 10 minutes before she'd reappear."

One day, Addie walked out of the yard and did not return. Amy and Steve scoured the neighborhood, but there was no trace of her. They put up flyers around town and posted notices online on local listservs and national lost pet sites.

Steve says they expected to find her. "She's a fairly big dog, and we thought she'd just return home on her own eventually. But as the days passed and there was nothing, we started to fear the worst. Then there was an e-mail."

The message came from a trucker who said he saw Addie limping by the side of a main road. Wanting to help, but unable to take an immediate detour to the vet, he picked her up and took her home with him to a neighboring state. Then he went online to a site that listed lost pet notices and saw Addie's picture.

"We were so relieved to find out that she was okay and felt really grateful that she'd been found by this man who obviously cared enough about animals to do the right thing. The guy said he'd taken Addie to the vet with a cut paw. He asked if we could reimburse him for the vet bill. Of course we said yes. We did ask that he send us a receipt from the vet, which he did. Where he lived was a six-hour drive from us. Steve offered to make the drive, but the man told us that he had a friend, a fellow trucker, who was coming our way and could bring Addie. The only thing was, he'd have to give the friend a little something by way of compensation. So altogether it came to $450. We had offered a reward for her return anyway, so we were happy to pay. Steve just did it online via PayPal."

On the appointed day, Amy and Steve waited anxiously for Addie's arrival. By evening, when no one had turned up, they tried contacting the man who said he'd found her, but they were unable to reach him. The next day, there was still no word.

"It doesn't immediately hit you that you've been conned," says Steve, "because there are other possibilities which seem more likely. Maybe there was a misunderstanding, maybe the guy got sidetracked, maybe Addie ran away again. I mean, who would scam someone over a lost pet?"

The truth sank in with Amy a little sooner. "When Addie didn't show up on time, I said right away that it was a hoax. That guy never had Addie. He never even saw her. He just saw our notice online and decided it was easy money. For all I know, he just went right down the line and contacted all the pet owners who had posted on that site. Never mind the fact that he'd got our hopes up about this dog that we loved. She used to lay herself down across the threshold of our baby's room like some kind of guardian angel. Now our daughter will never know her. The fact that someone could milk that loss for personal gain is truly disturbing."

GONE PHISHING

Joel is a big soccer fan. He played in high school and college and continues to play in an amateur league on weekends. He follows his city's Major League Soccer (MLS) team with enthusiasm, despite their underwhelming performance. So when it came time for soccer's World Cup, he was, as he admits, counting down the hours until the first match.

While at work, he received an e-mail from his MLS team. This was not unusual. As a season ticket holder, he was on their e-mail list and regularly received updates and messages.

"This one said that with the World Cup coming up, they were offering subscribers a chance to win some special World Cup memorabilia if they made a donation to the team's foundation. The foundation funds soccer programs for youths and does other good work in the community. I got my start in a program just like that when I was a kid, so I thought it was a good idea. Plus, I really wanted some of that World Cup gear. I clicked on the link to donate and it took me to a page that looked just like the team's page. It had their logo up top and photos of the team. So I put in my credit card information and made a $25 donation."

Joel went back to work feeling like he'd done his good deed for the day. The next morning there was another e-mail from the club waiting in his inbox. "I got a little excited. I thought maybe they were writing to inform me that I'd won the memorabilia."

Instead, the message contained bad news. "It was a fraudulent e-mail warning. The message that I'd received the day before was a fake. It said that if we got the e-mail, we should not click on any links and delete it immediately. If, like me, you'd provided personal information, you were advised to contact your financial institutions. As soon as I read it, I had a sick feeling in my stomach."

When Joel called his credit card company, the customer service representative confirmed that in the last 24 hours, charges of $2,200 had posted to his account. "He said that normally with that kind of activity, they would contact me to make sure these were authorized charges. But I beat them to the punch. The charges were for things like a TV, computers, and digital cameras. The customer service rep told me that they could work to resolve the charges, but that any personal information I'd provided could also be used to open new accounts in my name, to create fake driver's licenses, passports, a whole slew of things. Then he tried to sell me his company's identity theft protection services. Too much."

The e-mail Joel received is an example of *phishing*, a favorite of identity thieves, who try to obtain personal information under false pretenses. It takes place when someone receives an e-mail or pop-up screen that claims to be from a legitimate source but is in reality fishing for identifying information. Anyone with an e-mail account has received a phishing message.

For example, it may be a message from your bank asking you to contact them to verify account details. The message will usually include a link to an imitation website where you will be asked to enter personal information that allows thieves to access your accounts and money. Sometimes these phishing messages are easy to spot (especially when they're from banks you've never heard of), but other times they can look very much like the real thing.

If they can't get your attention by scaring you, they might appeal to a person's greed. A phishing e-mail sent to Dallas residents informed them they were eligible for a tax rebate. The e-mail directed them to a fake website where they were asked to provide Social Security numbers and other personal details. The good news is that phishing is pretty easy to avoid by simply ignoring the bait.

Spear phishing is a highly targeted form of phishing that customizes or personalizes e-mails to a degree that they are almost indistinguishable from the real thing. Spear phishers are aimed at specific segments of people, for example, everyone who works at a certain company or members of an online community. These e-mails often address the recipients by name and can look like they came from the person in the next cubicle. The people who targeted Joel were aiming at the supporters of that particular team and were able to craft the message accordingly.

LOVE FOR SALE

"It was my daughter who got me into online dating. She said I should really get out there and meet someone, but at my age, really, what are the options for meeting a nice guy? I'm not very outgoing, I live in a small town, and I work full-time."

Delia is divorced with two grown daughters. Although she has a computer at home, she only used e-mail sporadically and rarely surfed the Web. Then her daughter Hazel showed her a magazine article about online dating.

"It talked about how older folks were also using the Internet to meet people. I started to think, hey, maybe it's not such a bad idea. I already had the computer. Might as well put it to some good use. Hazel set me up with an account on one of the dating sites. We worked on my profile together. I said I was just looking for friendship, which was true. She took a photo of me and we put it up there. I never expected anything to come of it. It was just some silly fun with my daughter."

Delia fielded a few e-mail inquiries from men she found lackluster. "One was a lot older than me. Another looked like a serial killer. I'm not kidding. There was another guy who I'm sure was nice enough, but his interests were completely different from mine. He was looking for someone to take cross-country RV trips with him. That's not me. I was starting to think the whole thing was a waste of time. Then bam, there was Jerry."

In Jerry's first message to Delia, he told her that he was an American working overseas. "He said he was from Oklahoma originally but had been working in the oil industry in the Middle East and Africa for several years. He was based in Cairo. He was a widower. What drew me to him in the first place was the personality that came across in his e-mails. He seemed really sweet and down to earth. He started off by saying that he spent a lot of time working, and since his wife died, he hadn't really had any companionship."

The two began an e-mail correspondence that quickly became romantic. They exchanged photos, letters, and text messages. They discovered that they had much in common, including faith. Both were devout Christians. Jerry had told Delia that phone conversations were difficult because of the time difference, but he did surprise her with a call on her birthday. Although she was out and unable to speak to him in person, she treasured his voicemail message.

"It was just amazing to hear his voice at last. I played it over and over again. Then on Valentine's Day, he sent flowers. My ex-husband never sent me flowers, not once in 24 years of marriage."

This continued on for months. The more she communicated with Jerry, the more Delia felt that there could be a future with him. "He was nearing retirement age and planning to come back to the States. We started talking about that, how we could continue the relationship after he returned. It's important to me to be close to my family, whereas he had no family obligations, so we discussed the possibility of him moving here to North Carolina. He said he had all this money saved up from working overseas. He wanted to spend it on me. He'd send me links to different things on the Web, like jewelry or clothes, saying, 'Do you like this? I'll buy it for you.' Honestly, he made me feel like a teenager again."

About six months into their romance, Jerry told Delia he was coming to the States to visit her but first needed help with a banking issue. He had been hired to do a consulting job and paid with money orders, which he was unable to cash. Would she deposit the money orders and send him the cash via wire transfer?

"I agreed to do it. The first one was for $150. I put it into my account and sent him the money. Then he sent three more, each for $500. I deposited those as well and wired him $1,500."

Meanwhile, Jerry told Delia he'd booked a plane ticket and would be flying in for two weeks. "I was overjoyed, so excited. I couldn't wait to introduce him to my daughters."

On the day before Jerry was scheduled to leave Cairo, Delia received a phone call from her bank. The money orders she had deposited were not legitimate.

"They said the paper was real money order paper, but that the amounts had been altered, from $5 to $500 each. I was shocked. I thought, my God, he's been cheated. His employers cheated him. I never thought once that he might be to blame. They said that I was responsible for the money I'd wired out, even though the money orders were fake. That was another shock."

Delia sent a text message to Jerry asking him to call her immediately. When he did, she gave him the bad news.

"He was upset, as I was. He apologized for the trouble it had caused me but promised he would pay me back for the money I'd lost. Then he said he was all packed and set to leave, but he had just found out he needed to pay some outstanding utility bills. All his money had already been transferred to his American bank. Would I be able to loan him some money temporarily?"

Delia explained that her account was now overdrawn because of the money order fiasco and she had no other funds. Jerry said he understood, but without the cash, he might have to delay his trip.

"That was a blow. I'd been looking forward to it so much. I think at that point I would have done anything to make sure he got here."

Delia said she'd find a way to get $500 to him right away. She put it on her credit card, figuring she would get the money back as soon as he arrived.

"I texted him to say the money was on the way. He wrote back, said he couldn't wait to see me and that he loved me." Her voice catches. "That was the last I heard from him."

Two days later, Delia went to the airport to meet her new love. Two hours after the flight landed, she was still waiting. She begged the airline representatives to check passenger lists on other flights, to no avail. "At first, I was worried. I thought something might have happened to him. There was nothing I could do but go home. I tried e-mailing and calling, but there was no reply. For days, I tried to get in touch with him with no luck."

Delia was distraught. Still believing Jerry was all he said he was, she thought maybe he'd gotten cold feet and changed his mind about her. It was her daughter Hazel who gently suggested that perhaps "Jerry," as she knew him, had never existed, and that he was a con man.

Hazel felt she was to blame for her mother's predicament. "After all," she says, "I was the one who suggested she go online. I felt terrible. It took a while to convince her that Jerry must have been a fraud. She couldn't wrap her head around the idea that he was a creation from start to finish. It was too cruel."

Finding a soul mate has never been easy. The Web offers the lovelorn a wealth of opportunities to search for and find that someone special. The circumstances under which Delia met Jerry are typical. The con artist contacts someone who is looking for friendship or romance through an online dating service. Sometimes using photos and profiles stolen from other online daters, the crook makes contact by e-mail, phone, or text message. He or she then spends time wooing the victim, sending gifts, and acting the part of the perfect companion.

These sweetheart scams abound. They always begin with the quick establishment of a relationship between the victim and perpetrator. The victims feel they have found the person of their dreams, someone who seems unbelievably kind and attentive. They talk or write often, even daily, until the perpetrator feels he or she can make a move. Then the requests start rolling in. It may start with cashing checks or money orders and escalate into outright pleas for money to cover travel or medical expenses or costs associated with some emergency or crisis. In one case, a woman claimed her son had been badly injured and asked for money to cover hospital bills.

WHAT'S THE 419?

One of the early e-mail scams is widely associated with cons that originated in Nigeria in the 1980s. Utilizing advance fee fraud, the Nigerian scam is known also as *419 fraud* after the section in the Nigerian penal code that corresponds to this type of crime.

The classic Nigerian letter con begins with a communication (originally letters, now e-mail messages) asking for help in transferring a large sum of money out of Nigeria in exchange for a percentage of the money. In order to participate, the victim is asked to provide bank account details and/or money to cover associated fees. Over time, variations on the scam have emerged.

Here is an excerpt from a current 419 e-mail making the rounds:

I am Mr. Wong Cheng, at the Bank of XXXX, United Kingdom Branch. I contact you today concerning an investment placed under our bank's management 6 years ago. Please keep the content of this E-mail confidential. In 2005, a Customer of ours informed us that he had a financial account of 4 million United States Dollars, which he wished to have us turn over (invest) on his behalf and I was nominated to take care of this investment. The investment has yielded a total sum of 8.35 Million USD.

In mid-2009, he asked that the money be liquidated because he needed to make an urgent investment requiring cash payments in Europe. He directed that I liquidate the funds and have it deposited with a firm. This was the last communication we had. Four days later, a person who suited his description was declared dead of a heart attack in the South of France.

Mr. Wong Cheng explains that no next of kin has been found for this dead customer and goes on to say that although what he is about to propose will "smack of unethical practices," he'd like to split the money with you, the e-mail recipient. All that he needs to do is to name you as the next of kin and the money will be released. He stresses that he is a family man and "not a criminal," but he cannot let this chance pass him by.

In some instances, the perpetrators use fake checks, claiming the checks represent a portion of the money, and asking the victim to wire back money for fees. In other cases, they ask for bank account details, supposedly in order to deposit the money. Once they have been paid, the criminals will continue to bombard the victim with requests for more and more money. Even if the victim eventually stops complying with the demands, the con artists can still use the bank account information supplied initially to empty the victim's bank accounts. At its worst, the Nigerian letter scam has led victims to travel to Nigeria, where they are subjected to harassment, intimidation, and even physical abuse.

Since its debut, the scam has expanded to include a variety of countries and scenarios. It may be the estate of a dead celebrity or money won in a huge lawsuit, but the basic outline remains the same. Someone somewhere has a lot of money and they want to give you some of it. All you need to do is to follow three easy steps. Open your wallet, remove cash, and hand it over.

PROTECTING YOURSELF

Use caution online. Online transactions are convenient, easy, and in most cases safe. However, as with the telephone, you should be initiating the activity. If you want to buy something online, type in the address yourself. Do not click on a link in an unsolicited e-mail message, even if it appears to be from a legitimate source.

Do not respond to unsolicited e-mail messages. These messages are automated and sent out as part of a mass spam mailing. Until you respond, they probably do not have your individual e-mail address. Think of the spam as the bait on a hook. If you bite, even to say no thanks, they are going to want to reel you in and may continue to write and harass you. This goes for all unsolicited e-mails from strangers.

Keep it under wraps. If you are doing online banking, many banks have added security precautions that help to keep your information private. Do not share your passwords with anyone. Avoid passwords that are obvious, such as your birth date or mother's maiden name. Change your passwords and update your anti-virus software regularly. Make sure you have installed the latest browser updates. Log out of and close secure sites when you have completed your transactions.

Do not post personal information on social networking sites or blogs. Sites such as Facebook or Twitter can give you a false sense of security because you feel you are among friends. Remember that whatever information you make available on these sites is available not only to your friends, but potentially to their friends and acquaintances, as well as to hackers. Consider it as closer to a public bulletin board than your personal chat room and you will be less likely to want to share sensitive information. Configure your privacy settings to limit the number of people who can see your information and postings.

Be an educated consumer. If the price for an item or a property seems unbelievably low, there's probably a reason why.

Don't accept overpayments. If you receive payment for a sum greater than the amount you are asking for, do not accept it. If the buyer refuses to provide correct payment, find another buyer.

Be wary of communications coming from overseas. Notices of overseas lottery winnings, foreign buyers or sellers or love interests, sudden windfalls involving strangers in faraway lands—all of these scream "scam." This doesn't mean that you can't be scammed by someone who lives next door, but a foreign contact combined with any one of the other signs of a scam will guarantee that the person is not to be trusted. Don't even bother responding.

Stay private when in public. Do not frequent secure websites via public wireless connections. If you are using your laptop in a public area and do not need to access the Internet, turn off your wireless connection.

Use common sense. Ask yourself if the transaction passes the smell test. Why would a complete stranger want to share $5 million with you? Why would they send a check for $15,000 when the rent is only $3,000? If an online classified ad lists a seller's location as Florida and then you are asked to send money overseas, walk away.

Less is more. If your pet goes missing and you post a flyer or an ad, keep at least one important detail to yourself. This will help you verify the pet's identity if someone claims to have found him or her.

(8)

OUT AND ABOUT

Sidestepping Street Swindles

Living in Minneapolis, Lonnie has endured his share of harsh winters and looks forward to sunny spring days when he can eat lunch on the plaza outside his office. One afternoon, Lonnie was finishing his lunch and contemplating a return to his desk when a woman sitting nearby spoke to him.

"She said something about how she'd love to stay outside all day. I agreed, and we both started to head our separate ways. At that moment, a man walked by. He was holding a wallet, which he said he'd just found on the sidewalk. He asked if it belonged to either one of us. We both said no. So he opened it up to check for identification. There was no ID, but he did pull out a big wad of cash. It was a stack of C-notes, $100 bills. I made a little joke about it being mine after all. They seemed as surprised as I was to see the money."

The woman suggested taking the wallet to the reception desk inside the closest building to see if anyone had reported it missing. "The guy said he would, but if we couldn't find the owner, he suggested we divide the money between the three of us. The woman and I looked at each other. What the hell? I was in. Who can't use a little extra cash? But the lady, she was suddenly suspicious. She was concerned he might just run off with all the money."

The woman asked the finder to leave the cash behind while he checked in the building. He agreed but asked for some good-faith money as collateral.

"She pulled $100 out of her own wallet. I don't usually carry much cash around with me, but I'd just been to the ATM. So I handed over another $100 of my own. Then the woman rummaged around in her purse and found an old envelope. She took the cash wad out of the lost wallet, put it in the envelope, sealed it, and gave it to me for safe-keeping. The man went off, leaving the two of us standing there. I was holding the envelope stuffed with money. A few minutes passed by. We made small talk. Then she began to wonder where the guy went. She needed to get back to work and so did I."

Finally, the woman said she'd go check on the man's progress. She told Lonnie to stay where he was in case the man returned. "I saw her head toward the same building he had gone into. More minutes passed. Then I started to wonder myself. I'd just given someone $100 of my own money. But I was holding an envelope of cash that could belong to anyone. It was three or four grand easily, probably more. Those two were nowhere to be seen. I was beginning to feel a little nervous. How long was I supposed to wait for them? I gave it another 10 minutes and then figured I'd done my duty. I put the money in my jacket pocket and headed back to the office."

Back at his desk, Lonnie surreptitiously opened the sealed envelope to count the money. Inside, he found 50 sheets of scrap paper cut in the shape of $100 bills. "They were cut perfectly. The top sheet looked like a color photocopy of a real $100 bill, but it was so realistic I would have had trouble telling it was a phony if it hadn't been blank on one side. I couldn't believe it. It was so calculated and cold blooded."

Lonnie fell prey to a classic street con known as the *pigeon drop*. The scam requires two accomplices and a victim (the "pigeon"). The man and woman, seemingly unknown to one another, were in fact working hand in hand to rob Lonnie. It's likely that they knew he had just been to an ATM and chose him for that reason. A lost wallet is a common prop in the pigeon drop scam, but there are other versions utilizing jewelry and other belongings. Not everyone responds. In order for it to work as planned, the victim must possess a measure of curiosity and greed. But Lonnie's reaction was a common one. For many people, the sight of unclaimed cash is irresistible. How many of us have found a coin on the ground and picked it up? What if it was a dollar bill? How about $20?

In the comfort of your own home, you have the option of not answering the doorbell or phone. You can delete a suspicious e-mail message. But when you're out and you're approached directly by a scam artist, getting rid of him or her will require a little more effort on your part. You will need to be firm, because in a face-to-face encounter, a crook will be especially persistent, possibly intimidating, potentially charming, or all of the above. Street scams may conjure up visions of rapscallions engaging in cheeky cons whose victims may actually deserve what's coming to them. The reality of the street con is quite the opposite.

Street cons are among the oldest in the book. In 1849, the *New York Herald* reported on a hustler named William Thompson who roamed the city, approaching victims in the street, and setting up a con that made use of the question, "Have you confidence in me to trust me with your watch until tomorrow?" Surprisingly, this brazen scam worked. People handed over their valuable watches. And the term "confidence man" lives on to this day.

Successful scams perpetrated in public are not usually as straightforward as Thompson's. They almost always involve a story that sounds improbable but includes a promise of some reward for you if you go along. In some cases, however, they play to an individual's better nature.

Eva is a college junior. One evening as she waited at a bus stop near campus, an older woman came up to her. Speaking in a thick accent, she introduced herself as Miriam.

"She seemed disoriented. She said she had recently arrived from South Africa to visit her nephew. She'd taken a cab from the airport, but she was certain the driver had overcharged her and dropped her off at the wrong place. I asked how much she'd paid. Miriam said he had asked for $100, so she had definitely been cheated. She'd left some of her belongings in the cab and didn't have the nephew's address or phone number on her. All she could remember was that the street name was a letter of the alphabet. This is Washington, D.C. There is a street for almost every letter of the alphabet. At that very moment, we were standing on O Street. It could have been anywhere."

Eva advised Miriam to go to the police, but she refused. "I didn't know what else to do, so I offered my cell phone and dialed directory assistance. Miriam managed to get her nephew's number and call him. They had a conversation in their own language, then she handed me the phone and said he wanted to talk to me. He thanked me for helping Miriam and said he'd given her his address. She would have to take a cab to his house. I asked him if there was any way he could come pick her up, but he said he didn't have a car and he was home with his sleeping baby."

Miriam was shaken up from her first cab ride and hesitant to take another. Eva, in an attempt to be reassuring, said she would take down the cab's license plate number in case there was any problem.

"She was still very nervous about it and told me she didn't feel safe carrying all her money with her in the cab. She wanted to leave the bulk of her money with me for safekeeping and arrange to pick it up after she had rendezvoused with her nephew. She practically begged, and even offered to pay me to do it. I refused the money but said I would help."

Miriam opened up her bag and pulled out a thick stack of cash wrapped in a rubber band. She insisted that the money would be safer if it was kept together with Eva's money. Eva, who had finished a waitressing shift earlier in the day, had all her tip money in her wallet.

"There was no way all of her money was going to fit in my wallet, so I pulled out all my bills. Miriam produced a big handkerchief, wrapped up my bills with her stash, and handed it back to me. I gave her my cell number and made sure she got into the cab. I told her to call me when she got to her destination. I wanted to make sure she got there safely. She said she would." Eva took the bus home and waited for Miriam's call.

"About an hour later, I started to get worried. What if she hadn't made it there? What if she ended up in the wrong place? I don't know why, but I felt some responsibility for her. She was an old lady in a strange place. If it had been my relative, I'd like to think somebody would be looking out for her too."

Eva gave it another half-hour before calling the cab company. She had the license plate of the taxi that had picked Miriam up, and after cajoling the dispatcher, she was finally able to track down the driver. He relayed through the dispatcher that he had dropped Miriam off at a Metro stop a mile from campus. It was a $5 cab ride.

"I was confused, but I thought maybe she'd decided to take the Metro instead. That made me worry even more. I didn't have the nephew's number because we'd gone through directory assistance and they connected us to the number automatically. I decided to check the handkerchief to see if a phone number or address had somehow made its way in there."

Inside the white handkerchief, Eva found a neatly wrapped bundle of newspaper pieces, cut to resemble bills. There was no sign of her tip money.

"It took a minute to sink in that she'd conned me. I reconstructed the whole scenario in my mind. She must have somehow pocketed my money while she was pretending to wrap it up in the handkerchief. The nephew, or whoever he was, was in on it too. She probably wasn't even from South Africa. I was so mad. I'd worked a whole shift and there was probably $150 in there. That's a lot of money to me. Wasn't there some millionaire they could hit up? Were they purposely looking for poor college students?"

Miriam's scam was the *handkerchief switch*, also known as the Jamaican switch or the South African switch. Eva experienced a relatively simple version of the con, which bears similarities to the pigeon drop. The basic premise of the handkerchief switch is that each person hands over an amount of money that is put in a hanky or envelope for safekeeping. Then a little sleight of hand ensues and the real money goes in their pockets while the victim is left with the fake bills. The backstory in a handkerchief switch differs from the pigeon drop. It will vary in complexity, but it usually includes a newcomer to this country who has a large sum of cash that needs to be protected in some way.

TICKET TO RIDE

Marisol was doing her weekly shopping at the grocery store when a man approached her and asked if she spoke Spanish. "He looked like my younger brother. He was clean cut, presentable. I answered him in Spanish. He said his name was Eduardo."

Eduardo needed help. He showed Marisol a Mega Millions ticket and said he believed it was a winner. He spoke no English. Could she call the lottery hotline number and check for him?

"I said sure. He dialed the number on his cell phone and gave the phone to me. I read out the numbers to the person who answered. She

congratulated me and said that the ticket was one of 37 tickets to win
$10,000."

Marisol gave the good news to Eduardo, who was happy, but sub-
dued. "I told him it wasn't the big jackpot, but hey, it was still a lot of
money."

Eduardo told her that he was an undocumented alien and there was
no way he could collect his winnings. He didn't want to be exposed and
risk arrest. Marisol asked if there was anything she could do to help.
Eduardo's face brightened.

"He wanted me to buy the ticket from him. At first, I refused. That
was his money. I didn't want to take advantage of him that way."

But Eduardo was insistent. He had to get back to El Salvador. His
wife was expecting their first baby and he had promised to be there for
the birth. He offered to sell the ticket to Marisol for $1,000, one-tenth
of its value. He assured her that she would be doing him a favor.

"I said I didn't walk around with that kind of money. But there was
a branch of my bank right there in the grocery store. He showed me a
photo of his wife on his phone. He asked me to think about how far a
thousand bucks will go in El Salvador. So I said I would do it."

Marisol withdrew the money from her savings account and gave it to
Eduardo. "He was very thankful. He kept saying, 'God will bless you.'
And then he left."

To claim her prize, Marisol discovered she would have to fill out a
claim form and send it in with the ticket. She handed the job over to
her teenage daughter.

"My daughter, she does everything online, so she went and looked
on the lottery site to get the form and address. She decided to double-
check the number to make sure we had got the amount right. That's
when she discovered that the ticket we had was not a winning ticket.
Well, no, I shouldn't say that. There was one number on it that matched.
So it was a $2 winner."

If the chances of you winning the lottery yourself are slim, the
chances of a real winner choosing you to split his winnings are absolutely
zero. In this scam, there is always some reason why the person cannot
cash the ticket on his or her own. Immigration status is a common ex-
cuse. Another is a lack of money to pay the "claim fee" (there isn't one).
Sometimes perpetrators will say they have an outstanding traffic viola-

tion or some other legal complication that prevents them from claiming the prize money. Those who are unable to get money out of the victims have been known to accept other forms of payment, such as watches, jewelry, or any other valuable items the victim can easily produce on the spot.

"I didn't understand," says Marisol, "because we had called to check the numbers. My daughter said, 'Who did you call?' I said it was the lottery office. She asked me who made the call, and I said it was Eduardo. She said, 'Mom, he probably just called a friend of his.' But he was looking at the ticket when he dialed the number, like he was reading it off the ticket. Every little thing was so convincing."

ROCKS IN A BOX

Owen had been helping a friend move to a new apartment. As he went in and out of the building with boxes, he noticed a young man standing next to a parked white van. The man was smoking a cigarette, looking around, but doing nothing in particular. He caught Owen's eye, nodded, and offered his cigarette pack. Owen, who didn't smoke, declined. Then the guy walked over to Owen.

He asked, "Hey man, are you moving in?"

Owen replied no, that he was just helping a friend.

"Oh. How about a housewarming present for your friend?" The man pointed toward his van.

"Housewarming present?"

"Or maybe just something for yourself. Come take a look."

Curious, Owen followed the man to his van. Inside were several boxes of name-brand electronics, including video cameras, digital cameras, and laptops.

"These are all new," the van owner said. "Excess inventory."

Owen was wary. "Excess inventory from where?"

The goods were acquired from a department store where his cousin worked, the man said. They were for sale at a substantial discount. It sounded dubious, but Owen didn't probe further.

Owen had been looking to buy a video camera. He'd had an idea percolating in his head to put together a video for his dad's 70th birthday.

In order to do so, he'd need a good-quality camcorder, and that had always seemed like an unnecessary luxury item. Still, there was no harm asking, he thought. He pointed to a Sony high-definition camcorder and asked the price.

"That is a prize item, my friend," said the man. "Full retail price is $500. You can have it for $200."

In his research on cameras, Owen had not seen that particular model on sale for anything less than $480. Even given the questionable origins of the camera, the price was astounding. The only problem was, he didn't have anywhere near that kind of money on him, and he told the seller so. The seller pointed helpfully to an ATM across the street. Owen said he had left his wallet at home and was carrying only a little bit of cash. How much cash, the seller wanted to know. Just $75.

"No way," the seller said. "I can't give it away. What about your friend over there?"

Owen's friend came up with an additional $40, bringing the total to $115. He made the offer to the van owner.

"He was completely disgusted, even spat on the ground," said Owen. "But in the end, he took the money. A small sale is better than no sale, I figured."

There was one open camcorder box with a camera that Owen had been able to inspect and fiddle with. The rest of the boxes were sealed. Owen took a sealed box and put it aside in his friend's apartment until they were done moving. When he finally arrived home later that evening, he sat down with the box in eager anticipation.

It looked completely new. The box was sealed securely, with no signs of tampering. Inside, the original packaging was intact. As Owen carefully began stripping away the different layers, he came to the cushioning insulation and lifted that off. There, nestled inside, was a colorful object. At first, he thought he'd bought a special edition camera with some sort of novelty design on it. Then he picked it up and realized it was something completely different. It was in fact a cleverly constructed papier-mâché replica of a camcorder filled with a lead weight.

This scam is known as *rocks in a box*. Victims think they're getting a great bargain and find they've purchased a box of rocks or something equally worthless instead. Owen was furious and felt like a fool. At the same time, he respected the ingenuity of the person who'd packed the box. They'd clearly taken care with it. Nevertheless, he'd lost $115 of his and his friend's money, and he was still nowhere closer to owning a video camera.

Making purchases at established retail outlets doesn't always guarantee that you will get what you pay for, but at least then you have a receipt. You can take the item back.

If buying something on the street conjures up images of a man in a trench coat lined with stolen watches, you're on the right track. Flea markets are one thing, but generally speaking, genuine deals are not found on the sidewalk. Big-ticket items like electronic equipment and gadgets are popular for the rocks in a box swindle because these products usually retail for hundreds or even thousands of dollars, and they are offered at prices that are hard to resist. Victims across the globe have been fleeced by offers of new laptops at deep discounts. In California, con artists convinced their targets that the boxes couldn't be opened for inspection because to do so would violate the warranty. Another victim got home to discover that the laptop bag contained not a top-end computer but potatoes. If the purchasers do not have cash on them, scammers will wait for them to return from the ATM or even accompany them to the bank.

If it occurs to you, as it did to Owen, that someone selling laptops out of a van most likely stole them, then it might not seem so strange that he or she wants to unload them for a low price. This is part of the rocks in a box scam—leading you to believe that you're getting a good deal. Even if it was true and the bag contained a real laptop instead of potatoes, you would still be involving yourself in a criminal enterprise. Purchasing goods you believe or know to be stolen is illegal.

FORTUNE-TELLING FLIMFLAM

Fortune-tellers are the Starbucks of scams. There seems to be one on every corner. Those neon signs promising a glimpse into your future are seductive. Although they advertise $5 palm readings for walk-in clients, victims can end up spending thousands of dollars to ensure their good fortune.

"Her name was Nadia. My friend Lynn had gone to her and said she was amazing."

Monique is 42. A mother of three, she is twice divorced and works as assistant manager at a grocery store. During a night out with girlfriends, she heard Lynn rave about Nadia's psychic powers.

"We were having a good time, we'd had a few drinks, so I said, if she's so good, let's see what she's got to say about me. That's how it started. It was all in fun."

Monique made an appointment with Nadia the following weekend. "She came to my house. Nadia said it would work better if she was surrounded by my things in my environment. It made sense."

Nadia was younger than Monique had expected, and more businesslike. "I had to pay her up front, $20. She walked through the house once and then we sat down at the kitchen table. The whole time she was deep in thought. I had expected something a little more lighthearted. Anyway, she took my hands, looked at them for a while on both sides. Then she took out a purple velvet scarf and laid it on the table, took out a deck of tarot cards, dealt five of them on the table. Then she shook her head, shuffled the cards, and dealt them out again. She still hadn't told me anything, and I was curious."

After dealing the second hand of cards, Nadia pulled her things together and said, "You are in great danger."

"Jesus, Mary, and Joseph. The way she said it sent chills down my spine. Here I am thinking she's going to say something like, 'You'll meet a tall, dark stranger.' Instead, she said there was someone in my family who was very ill. That was true; my mother was suffering from breast cancer. Nadia said that evil forces were also trying to hurt my family. She asked if I had any enemies. Well, I'm not on good terms with either of my ex-husbands, so I mentioned them, but only jokingly."

Nadia said something or someone was filling the house with destructive energy. If Monique did nothing, she or her children would come to harm.

"She explained that someone had placed a curse on us. I said, 'A curse? Come on.' But she was deadly serious. She said it was like someone had released a rattlesnake into our house. It was dangerous and hidden and would eventually harm someone. If I had a rattlesnake in the house, wouldn't I want it removed? It was the same with the curse. And she could remove it for us."

Monique was doubtful, especially after Nadia quoted a curse removal fee of up to $1,000, depending on the strength of the curse. "I told her I'd have to think about it. It was a lot to take in all at once, and it wasn't a small amount of money."

Nadia told Monique she was making a mistake, and that with every passing day, the curse would grow in strength. "She told me to watch out for bad omens and said she'd call in three days to check on me. Then things did get weird. The first day, I found a dead bird on the lawn. The second day, I locked my keys inside my car. And the third day, my son, who's 11, was injured in a soccer game. I couldn't say for sure, but all three of those things seemed to qualify as bad omens."

Nadia's call came right after Monique returned home from the emergency room with her son. "I said she was right; there was something strange going on. I asked her to come out to the house."

Nadia returned. She told Monique she would charge $120 to "read" the house and determine the extent of the curse. Then she would be able to quote a price for the actual removal.

"She took out the same purple scarf she'd had the first time and put it over her head. She lit some incense, which she said was to enhance her abilities. Then she walked around the house for about 10 minutes, came back to the kitchen, and told me it would be $750 to remove the curse. By that time, I was feeling completely creeped out."

Monique agreed to have Nadia remove the curse. Nadia told her she and her family had to be out of the house in order for the ritual to work. They left, with instructions to return two hours later.

"When we got back, Nadia said she had performed the removal ceremony and the house was cleansed of evil, but we would need regular monthly blessings in order to keep it that way."

Having already paid a hefty fee to have her house exorcised, Monique decided prevention was better than a cure and went ahead with the monthly blessings, at $150 each. But Nadia wasn't done with her yet.

Two months later, Monique's mother went into decline and had to enter a hospice. Not long afterward, she died. On the one-month anniversary of the death, Nadia showed up at Monique's house and said she sensed a restlessness of spirit that she attributed to Monique's mother's passing. "She asked me if my mother had left anything to me, like mementos or money. I said she'd left it all, the house, all her possessions, everything."

Nadia said she had a bad feeling. She asked Monique for an egg and then a bowl. Monique complied. Nadia tapped the egg on the side of the table and cracked it open into the bowl. Out came the egg white, yolk, and what looked like a feather and a fragment of bone. There was also a drop of something resembling blood.

"I screamed and jumped out of my chair," says Monique. "It was disgusting. Nadia said it was a warning from the other side, from my mother. She said the bad spirits that had been in my home had infiltrated my mother's house and things. To remove them permanently, Nadia would need $100 for each year of my mother's life. Only then could my mother's soul rest in peace."

Monique, who had been very close to her mother, was alarmed. "It probably sounds crazy to any outsider, but I was in a bad way. I'd been having trouble sleeping since my mother died. I thought it might be related to these bad spirits Nadia was talking about. My mother suffered a lot at the end of her life, and the idea that she wasn't at peace even in death weighed heavily on me. So I paid. My mother died at 78, so it was $7,800."

In the end, Monique was rescued from Nadia's clutches not by a concerned friend or relative but by a development that took Monique completely by surprise.

"I was watching the local news one evening and there was a story about a fortune-teller who had been arrested for conning an old lady out of her life's savings. I looked up at the TV and there was a shot of Nadia, being hauled away in cuffs. I was stunned, totally blindsided. The story sounded familiar. She had befriended this older woman and convinced her she had been cursed. Over a period of months, the woman gave Nadia money that Nadia was supposed to purify and return to her. Eventually the woman's daughter caught on and asked her mom why her bank accounts were so low. The mother couldn't remember how much money she'd given Nadia, but the daughter figured it was about $150,000. Hearing that made me realize I'd probably gotten off lucky. She would have kept going until she'd taken everything I had."

As far as psychics go, good news doesn't pay as well as bad news. Claiming the victim or her family is under some kind of curse that only the fortune-teller can remove is a very common scheme. Removal of the curse will invariably involve money, and lots of it. Another tactic is to tell you that someone you know is going to fall ill or have an accident if you don't pay up. Now the fate of another person is in your hands. If victims are short on cash, fortune-tellers will take credit cards, jewelry, or whatever valuable items are available. One psychic even had a victim clean her house in lieu of payment.

Self-proclaimed seers are some of the most pernicious con artists around. They specialize in preying on the weak and vulnerable—the elderly, the unhappy, the unemployed, even the terminally ill. People who seek out fortune-tellers in a serious way are generally looking for some way to improve their lives. What they get instead is someone who will bleed them dry.

Psychics will use props to frighten their victims and up the ante. The egg ritual Monique experienced is a favorite. An egg is cracked, and blood, hair, or some other foreign substance is found inside. This supposedly signifies that an evil presence is at work. In reality, it is nothing more than a simple magic trick using sleight of hand and misdirection. Special "anti-curse" candles are also popular and, of course, expensive.

THE STREET BEAT

Devon and Brianne have run a number of street scams, including the pigeon drop, rocks in a box, and the lottery ticket swindle. They are young, able-bodied, and clearly possess some skills, but it has never occurred to them to seek out a more honest line of work. They deny that they are thieves, insisting that they are more akin to hustlers, trying to live by their wits.

"Look," says Devon, "I can turn on the TV any day of the week and see people playing poker. They bluff, they misrepresent, they take your money. Sometimes you win, sometimes you lose. It's all in the game. Life is a gamble."

Brianne agrees. "You think it's easy, what we do? It ain't easy. We're good at it."

The couple's favorite scam is *lost and found*, a variation on the pigeon drop that involves a found item, in their case, a piece of jewelry. Usually carried out at restaurants, gas stations, or rest stops, the scam begins with Brianne entering the establishment.

"I come in all upset, looking around. I tell the cashier or hostess that I've lost my engagement ring and ask if anybody's found it. She checks the lost and found and says no. I start crying and say that it's a 1-carat diamond, it's really valuable, my fiancé is going to give me hell. I've got to find it. I give her a phone number and ask her to call me if it turns up. I'm offering $500 as a reward. So right away she knows it must be worth way more than that."

"A little while later, I come in," says Devon. "I buy a soda or look at the menu or whatever. Then I pretend to discover a ring on the ground. It's actually hidden in my pocket. I take it to the cashier and tell her I found the ring. She will usually tell me that someone was looking for it earlier. Then I say there's probably a reward."

The cashier has already heard from Brianne that the ring is expensive. "The cashier has Brianne's phone number, but I'm the one who found the ring, so I say, how about we call the owner and split the reward? The only thing is, I'm on my way to work and I can't hang around long. Nine times out of 10, the cashier will offer to buy me out of my share of the reward. It's not unusual for them to offer me a hundred bucks. They're thinking one of two things. Either they're going to call Brianne and tell her they found the ring, or they're planning on selling the ring. Either way, they think they'll make a nice profit."

Except that the phone number Brianne provided is a phony, the ring turns out to be worthless, and they've just given Devon $100.

"Many times, if it's a cashier, they'll just reach into the cash register and pull out the money. I guess that'll cause some problems down the line if they can't make it right with the boss. Once, a hostess in a restaurant went around collecting money from her coworkers until she had enough."

Brianne and Devon keep a box of imitation rings handy for this purpose. Do they feel bad at all? "About what?" Brianne laughs.

This blatant amorality makes it possible for people like Devon and Brianne to operate freely without any pangs of conscience. Con artists, at least those who make a lifestyle of it, have no concern for other people's losses or suffering. It simply doesn't factor into their thinking. It's difficult for anyone with a conscience to understand, which can make it even easier for conners to operate. Marisol, the unlucky lottery scam victim, was bewildered as to why anyone would choose to make money by cheating others.

"As it was happening, the only thing that didn't feel right was that I was taking his lottery ticket. I never thought he might be fooling me, because how can you look someone in the eye and do that to them? I just hope that he really did have a wife and baby in El Salvador. Maybe that much was true. Maybe he was just desperate to make some money and get back to them. Otherwise, it's just plain evil."

While Marisol tries to extract some small consolation from her ordeal, the fact is that rather than heading home, the man who swindled her was probably on to the next store and the next victim within the hour.

Brianne finds the street work provides her with a rush of adrenalin. "It's kinda touch and go, because there are cops on the street. You have to be careful. There have been times when we've had to run for it, literally. It's a challenge every time. Will the person fall for it? There's a moment there when you can almost see them weighing the options in their mind. Then you see them decide one way or the other. If they go for it, you've succeeded, and there's a satisfaction to it. If not, it's definitely a letdown. Not to mention a waste of time."

Street cons can be difficult to dodge because the perpetrators are literally in your face. There is also an ambush-like quality that takes people by surprise. Firmness, vigilance, caution, and an awareness of the characteristics of a street con are essential to defending yourself. Con artists who interact personally with the public need to engage their targets quickly, assess their vulnerability, and implement their plan.

PROTECTING YOURSELF

Do not talk to strangers. Remember what your mother told you? If a stranger approaches you in public, say you're not interested and walk on. A quick rebuff or rejection early on is a good deterrent. The maxim "You can't con an honest man" is untrue, but a disinterested man or woman is a different matter.

Do not hand over money. This may seem obvious, but admit it, you've given change to a panhandler at least once in your life, haven't you? Do not give any money to strangers, even if you think you'll get it back. You won't.

Don't rely on an innocent bystander. Remember, many street cons use coconspirators who pretend not to know one another. Just because they appear to be acting like strangers does not mean that they are. Assume that if more than one person approaches you, they are in it together, which means that anything either one of them says will be designed to rip you off. The second person is often there to provide corroboration or to make you feel more comfortable giving the first person your money.

Hands off! Don't let anyone touch your wallet, your bag, or anything else of yours even for an instant. Keep your valuables with you at all times. Con artists are skillful with their hands. Your money will be in their pocket before you've even blinked. Similarly, don't take anything from them. In short, don't interact with them at all.

Safety in numbers. Avoid being alone in deserted places, especially after dark. If you leave an establishment on your own and someone in the parking lot tries to spin you any kind of yarn, don't lead them to your car. Go back inside and alert the management or call the police. If you are at an ATM and someone attempts to converse with you, leave or go inside the bank.

Stick to stores. Don't buy anything from an individual on the street. If you buy an item from a reputable retailer, you have the protection of warranties, returns, and exchanges. If you buy a camcorder from a man in a parking lot, you have a box of potatoes—if you're lucky. There's a reason why the seller is on a curb rather than behind a counter, and it isn't a good reason. Even if you do find a real camcorder in your box, you're participating in their illegal activity.

Be street smart. When strangers engage you in public with a story, they're almost always looking to scam you. Consider any approach suspect. This goes for something as simple as someone picking up a ring and saying, "Did you drop this?" to someone asking for directions. This doesn't mean that every tourist who asks for directions is a scam merchant, but the minute something of value is introduced (lost jewelry, a found wallet, a briefcase), this will be your cue to walk away.

Don't be greedy. Greed is the primary motivating factor for many scams, so if you haven't worked for it, you don't want it. If you want to play the lottery, buy your own ticket.

Shun psychics. If you're interested in knowing your future, buy a Magic 8 Ball. It will be cheaper and less painful. At their best, psychics are entertainers. At their worst, they're parasites. At no point are they actually able to divine the future, despite what anybody tells you. If you need someone to talk to, go to a friend or relative, not Madame Zizi.

Get the police. If someone comes up to you claiming to be in distress or needing help, offer to contact the police. Then see how fast they run.

⑨

DON'T MIX
BUSINESS WITH PLEASURE

Affinity Fraud and Investment Scams

The audio on the low-budget DVD is rough, but the message is clear. Here's a revolutionary product that will help you lose weight. The camera cuts to a small bottle filled with brown powder. Simply sprinkle it on whatever food you're eating and watch the pounds drop away. And on top of that, how would you like to get paid to spread the word? Stock images of luxury cars, mansions, and tropical island vacations flit across the screen. "Tired of living paycheck to paycheck? Your day has come," a voice intones. The implication? You're about to become a millionaire.

Tami lives in a small town near the Texas-Louisiana border. She first heard about the miracle powder, called Lose Enz, through her sister-in-law Patrice, who had been given the scoop by a coworker. Lose Enz, so called because it was supposedly derived from an enzyme that speeds up metabolism, was the brainchild of two Houston-based entrepreneurs. The pair touted their weight-loss aid at free seminars across the country, including one in Shreveport attended by Tami and Patrice. After the infomercial was over and the box lunches eaten, the company's founders, Mark and Silas, appeared on stage.

"There were probably 50 people there," said Tami, "but the way they came on, it was like they were at a revival in front of thousands. Silas did a short talk on the powder, explaining how it helped people lose weight. There were diagrams and statistics, before and after photos of people who had lost weight with it. But Mark did most of the talking. It seemed like he was the marketing guy and Silas was more of the product development guy."

Mark told attendees that they had a unique chance to get in on the ground floor of a huge, moneymaking endeavor. Lose Enz was going to transform the weight-loss industry. It was guaranteed to bring them a six-figure income within a matter of months. All they had to do was to bring more people into the fold.

Patrice describes the event. "Mark was yelling, 'Who wants to be a millionaire? Who's ready to get real?' And people started getting pumped up. By the end, we were all hollering."

Tami agrees. "What woman hasn't had weight issues? I couldn't tell you the number of diets I've been on myself. Patrice too. This felt like a win-win for us. It was a product we could actually get behind."

After watching the pitch, Tami and Patrice decided to take Mark and Silas up on their offer to become Lose Enz dealers. The startup cost was $500 apiece for the most basic package. Rather than selling the product, however, participants were told that they would get paid simply to tell others about the miracle powder.

"Even better," says Patrice. "We could make money just by telling friends and family about it. We would be paid a commission for each person we could recruit to become a dealer. Between the two of us, we know a lot of folks."

To get the $500, Tami went to a payday lender and got a cash advance on her next paycheck. Patrice dipped into the money she and her husband had been saving for a new refrigerator. After paying out the startup fee, they both received small product samples and signed up for the training program.

Tami looked forward to getting started. "We each got two small bottles like the size of aspirin bottles. To get more, we had to enroll in a program where we'd receive monthly shipments and be billed automatically. In the meantime, we were scheduled to take part in two or three conference calls with the company's top trainers, who would provide all the information we'd need to go out there and recruit others."

The first conference call was a hype-filled session with the trainer telling participants that they could expect to see big changes in their lives immediately. He gave them tips on approaching potential recruits, provided them with talking points, and emphasized the need to be aggressive and quick in their recruiting strategies.

"The guy was like a drill instructor on speed," says Tami. "It was all about recruiting and how rich this was going to make us. He was talking about developing prospects, conversion rates, up selling. I had no idea what he was talking about, but I was excited. I'd always worked for somebody else. This was a chance for me to get something going myself. And I'm pretty outgoing, so I knew I'd be good at it."

The trainer also advised trainees that they would need the proper marketing tools to be successful. The infomercial was made available for $35 in DVD format and $50 as an electronic file that could be e-mailed and uploaded to the Web. Business cards were offered at $40 per thousand. Tami and Patrice invested in all of these. Then they began to give informal presentations to family, friends, and acquaintances. Many were interested, but only a few were able to come up with the $500 required to become distributors. Still, the two women were optimistic, certain that once they received a full shipment of powder and could show people how effective it was, business would pick up.

"How long did we wait?" Tami tries to recall.

"We signed up in August, and by October we still hadn't received anything," Patrice says.

"Right. We tried to get in touch, but there was no phone number on the website. We hadn't even noticed that before. So we e-mailed but got no response."

Meanwhile, payments kept piling up on their credit cards. Tami called her credit card company and was told she needed to contact the biller to request a stop to the automatic charges. To make matters worse, because she had borrowed money from a payday lender at exorbitant interest rates and had been unable to repay her original debt, she had taken out additional loans. As a result, she now owed the lender thousands of dollars.

After trying to contact the company for a month, the two women decided they might have better luck in person.

"We had an address," says Tami, "so we just got in the car and went." At the end of the four-hour drive, they pulled up outside the address they had printed out from the Lose Enz site. "When we got there and

I saw where we were, my heart just sank. Both of us just sat in the car and didn't say anything for a couple of minutes."

The location turned out to be a pack and ship store that rented out mailboxes.

"We didn't know what to do. We'd driven all this way and we still hadn't found anyone to speak to." Both women were still hopeful that the program would work out.

"We had a lot riding on it. Tami and I had already shelled out all this money. We'd signed up four or five people. We were still on board. We just wanted our commissions and product. If there was a manufacturing delay or something, we could work with it. All they had to do was let us know what was going on. It was really frustrating."

"The mailbox thing was weird, but after we thought about it, we decided they're on the road so much, maybe it's not worth it to rent out a place. Maybe that's why they don't have a phone either. We turned around and went home."

Back home, the women regrouped. They still had their small sample bottles of powder and decided to try a case study to prove their product's worth. A real live subject could provide testimonials and improve their sales pitch. They chose Patrice's husband, Darryl, who was Tami's brother.

"Darryl's always been overweight, ever since we were kids," says his sister. "He was happy to help, especially when we told him all he had to do was sprinkle this powder on whatever he ate. The very first time he tried it was on a sandwich. He said it tasted familiar. We told him they use flavorings to make it taste good. He said no, it tasted like something else. About the third time he tried it, he said, oh, I know what it is. It tastes like au jus. Like they serve with a French-dip sandwich. Patrice and I were like, whatever, Darryl, keep eating."

Darryl weighed in twice a day, in the morning and in the evening. Tami and Patrice kept detailed records of what he ate, how much, and all his measurements. At the end of two weeks, all their powder was gone, and instead of losing weight, Darryl had actually gained weight.

"That's when Tami and I really started to get depressed. We'd each spent about $1,500. Tami's bills were going up by the second, because she'd gone to that lender. The automatic payments were somehow still being charged to our credit cards. And we had nothing, nada. What's worse is that we'd managed to convince some of our relatives and friends to sign up, so they'd lost money too. That was awful, really awful."

Unbeknownst to them, the sisters-in-law had become ensnared in a *pyramid scheme*. Like any classic pyramid scheme, the Lose Enz swindle played on the desire to make an easy buck by investing in "a sure thing." Rather than striking it rich, however, participants find themselves striking out, losing much or all of their investment. As the old saying goes, if something looks too good to be true, it probably is, particularly where money is concerned. Many people would like to strike it rich overnight, but there's a reason why they don't. It's not easy. Any person who makes it sound like they've found a surefire way to make you an instant millionaire should immediately arouse suspicion.

So what are pyramid schemes? Presented as business opportunities, pyramid schemes require participants to pay an initial fee to become involved. In return, they are promised large commissions for recruiting new members to the operation. Each person they recruit must bring in a certain number of new people, and for each recruit, the original recruit receives a payment. As each new level of recruits is added on, the structure takes on the shape of a pyramid, with people paying out to their "upline," individuals further up the pyramid.

The premise usually involves the sale of a product, but unlike legitimate organizations, companies or individuals engaged in pyramid schemes do not sell their products to the general public. Rather, when sales do take place—and they don't always—the products are sold to other members of the pyramid scheme, who are often required to buy large amounts of inventory.

Pyramid schemes should be distinguished from multilevel marketing (MLM), which is not illegal and does involve selling a specified product to the public. In multilevel marketing enterprises, sellers receive payment for product sales and not for the recruitment of new salespeople. This is not to say that MLM programs are completely straightforward; they too often involve aggressive sales and marketing tactics and impose strict requirements on participants, but they manage to stay on the right side of the law.

As part of their pitch, Mark and Silas made sure to mention to audiences that they would be selling to their friends and neighbors. This made the whole project more comfortable for people like Tami and Patrice,

who are not professional salespeople but have access to a large and receptive network of people. In a pyramid scam, the initiators delegate a
portion of their dirty work to others who are unfortunately unaware of
what they are doing. Tami and Patrice certainly never intended to cheat
anyone, but by bringing in people they knew, they were responsible for
spreading the scam. In doing so, they entered the murky world of *affinity fraud*.

Affinity fraud targets members of the same social, religious, ethnic,
or other distinct group, which means that the very people sharing a
pew with you or sipping drinks at your club may be looking to bilk you.
Watching out for strangers is hard enough work, but caution should also
be exercised when dealing with those we know.

This kind of fraud works because people tend to be more trusting of
and more comfortable with someone who is like them in some way. A
sense of bonding and shared experience comes along with that common
affinity. For the con artist, there is also the added benefit of free publicity. Once a person is hooked, he or she is likely to spill the beans to
another member of the group.

SPINNING THE YARN

Maurice served as the figurehead in a family-run investment scheme
that also featured son Keith and daughter-in-law Carrie. The Judsons,
as they called themselves, posed as successful real estate investors and
traveled throughout the Pacific Northwest, enticing victims with promises of large returns on land deals. All three were eventually arrested,
but not before running through $5.2 million of other people's money.

Despite his conviction, Maurice doesn't admit guilt, but he is happy
to talk about his victims' shortcomings. "People are hungry for opportunity. They want to believe. We come along with something unique,
something that could take them to the next level. The problem is, they
don't want to hear about risk. And without risk, there is no reward."

On the face of it, the Judsons's strategy involved the purchase of large
tracts of land in Alaska. Keith and Carrie ran day-to-day operations,
which included pitches to investors. Claiming Maurice was a Korean
War veteran, the trio targeted veterans' groups, telling audiences that

there was plenty of land up north that could be bought on the cheap and sold for a fortune to oil companies seeking new drilling fields.

"We bought them lunch, told them the story, and they were lining up to be a part of it, that one last adventure. And damn right. It was a great idea," says Maurice.

Whether or not it was a great idea, the truth is that it was simply untrue. Investors were shown photos of beautiful Alaskan landscapes taken from back issues of *National Geographic* and told that it was land they now owned. Victims were allowed to buy in for a minimum investment of $5,000, but some gave six-figure amounts. They were also promised a charter flight to Alaska to check out their new land.

When confronted with the facts, Maurice is adamant that no deception was intended, that he is nothing more than an unlucky businessman. "Have you been to Alaska? It's stunning. We had prime parcels of land. We had an amazing trip lined up for our folks. Glaciers, fishing, you name it. But some things are out of your control. We had some deals fall through. What can I say?"

Even from behind bars, Maurice manages to sound sincere. It is easy to see how he was able to manipulate hundreds into giving him money. It is also easy to forget that there was never any plan to purchase land, no trip, no investment opportunity. The money went straight from investors' bank accounts into the pockets of the Judsons. Police doubt any of the three had even been to Alaska. They simply took an issue from the headlines— oil dependence—and came up with a creative way to use it as a hook.

As part of the case against them, investigators documented how the Judsons spent the money they were given. All of the money was spent on personal goods or services, including shopping sprees at designer boutiques, cars, Caribbean vacations, entertainment systems, parties, jewelry, and fine wine. Maurice and Keith also spent tens of thousands of dollars on guns and hunting trips.

Nora, the lead prosecutor, points out that Maurice is the only one of the three swindlers to comment on the case. "The other two have kept quiet, but Maurice just loves the sound of his own voice. You can see why; he's a charming man. He's all smiles and denials. He'll tell you that he was actually trying to help these people by giving them a shot at a real moneymaker. If I didn't know better, I'd say he believes it himself. But I do know better. I've visited with his victims, and I can assure you, they're not smiling. Some of them are living hand to mouth. One of these guys, when we were interviewing him, asked if Maurice was even a real Korea vet. I had to say no, because he wasn't. There was no record of him ever serving in the armed forces. Well, this old guy just couldn't get over it, that a person would lie about something that to him is near sacred. I tried to tell him, look, we're talking about a con man, but that was beyond the pale as far as he was concerned. It was one thing to lie about money, but that brotherhood forged in war, you just don't mess with that."

As it turns out, Maurice is a serial offender. The Alaska land deal is not his first con, or second, or third. "We uncovered a trail of complaints across half the United States dating back 40 years. Many of his scams had to do with real estate, but he also sold phony stocks and bonds. He was into a smoking cessation scheme for a while, where he sold kits that were guaranteed to help people quit. His very first con, or at least the first one we were able to track down, also played on the Korean War angle. He claimed that during his tour in Korea, he'd stumbled on a goldmine. He offered investors a stake in the mine in return for capital to develop it. I don't know if you'd call him a successful con man, but he was good at keeping one step ahead of the law. Whenever he ran into trouble, he charmed his way out of it, or said he'd suffered injuries in the war that affected his judgment. Many times he'd offer restitution and his victims would accept and leave it at that. His son and daughter-in-law are nowhere as skilled as he is, but they're possibly even greedier. If it hadn't been for them wanting to perpetrate this scam, Maurice might have retired and never been caught."

ROBBING PETER TO PAY PAUL

Pyramid and Ponzi schemes are the two most common forms of affinity fraud. The Ponzi scheme, made infamous by Italian immigrant Charles Ponzi in the 1920s, also relies on recruiting, but unlike a traditional pyramid operation, there is no product and no commission for recruiting. Instead, in a typical Ponzi scam, the con artist presents potential investors with a phony investment opportunity and promises them an extravagant rate of return on their money.

Because there is no real investment opportunity, the perpetrator pockets a portion of the money and uses the rest to pay off other investors. This last point is important, because it is responsible for both the success and the eventual failure of the Ponzi scheme. The success of a Ponzi con lies in its ability to fool people into thinking it's *actually working*. If you've paid into an investment and you start to receive money back, you are a happy investor. This method of "robbing Peter to pay Paul" ensures that Paul will remain your best friend as long as the payments keep coming.

Charles Ponzi's swindle is the textbook example. Ponzi, a charming and resourceful ex-con, hatched a scam in 1919 involving international reply coupons, essentially prepaid postage coupons that could be used around the world. As Ponzi explained to his clients, his investment involved a complicated plan to take advantage of price discrepancies by buying the coupons on the cheap overseas and redeeming them for a profit in the United States. He promised investors that he could double their money in three months, a remarkable feat.

Many of his early investors were, like him, Italian immigrants. They trusted Ponzi and found his proposal irresistible. The money began pouring in, and Charles Ponzi began living the high life. Many of his investors were persuaded to reinvest rather than cashing in their profits. When they did ask to be paid, he simply used money from other investors to cover the payments. For a time, the scheme prospered. Hopeful investors, large and small, lined up to put their money into Ponzi's hands.

In the end, however, Ponzi's plan was doomed, as is the case with all pyramid and related cons. Ultimately, the debts will always exceed the profits. Moving money around can only go so far. At the beginning, incoming funds can cover occasional payments to investors, but as the number of investors grows, the elaborate juggling act that is the pyramid or Ponzi scheme will inevitably fail. Increasing scrutiny from the media and the authorities finally led to Charles Ponzi's arrest and imprisonment on charges of fraud. He eventually left the United States and died a pauper in Rio de Janeiro.

THE IMITATOR

Charles Ponzi was not the first to initiate a bogus investment scheme, and he certainly was not the last. In one of the most high-profile cases of all time, New York fund manager Bernard L. Madoff was accused of perpetrating a $50 billion scam affecting thousands of individuals, non-profits, foundations, and educational institutions.

Madoff, once a respected Wall Street financier, was found guilty of maintaining an elaborate international Ponzi scheme disguised as a highly convoluted investment fund that no one but he could understand. In 2008, as the U.S. economy began its downward spiral and investors began looking to pull out their cash, the entire operation fell apart. It was later discovered that in true Ponzi fashion, Madoff had not actually bought any stock with his clients' money. After the swindle came to light, victims confessed that they had never really understood the financial statements provided to them by Madoff but simply assumed everything was above board because their investments, at least on paper, were thriving.

Among Bernard Madoff's clientele were a number of Jewish organizations and members of the same exclusive organizations to which Madoff himself belonged, including his country club. Hungry would-be investors happily paid the hefty membership dues in hopes of gaining an introduction to the legendary Bernie Madoff.

BIRDS OF A FEATHER

Geeta is an active member of a tight-knit South Indian Christian community in New Jersey. She heads her church's Sunshine Committee, which provides meals and other services for congregants who are homebound, whether through illness, childbirth, or infirmity. She and her husband, Naveen, are regular contributors to the church's mission in India, and they regard their fellow churchgoers as extended family members.

When her friend Ashna's son Rohit returned from a trip to India, the two families gathered at Geeta's home for a weekend meal. Rohit had news to share. While in India, he told them, he had met up with a cousin whose business was developing telecommunications systems in rural areas. The cousin had invited Rohit to come see the work that was being done, and Rohit was very impressed by what he saw. His cousin then asked Rohit if he would like to invest in the business. Rohit, still in his early 20s, hadn't been able to save much money yet. He agreed to make a small financial commitment and promised to try to find investors back in the United States.

Naveen's interest was peaked. He invited Rohit to come back the following day to continue the conversation. When Rohit returned, he came bearing gifts.

Geeta describes the visit. "He gave us copies of different reports that talked about the benefit of telecommunications to rural villages, along with clippings from Indian newspapers about mobile phone this, wireless that. He was very enthusiastic about it all. He said if we got involved, we could really make a difference in the lives of these villagers."

"Sending money back to India was not new for us," says Naveen. "We had been supporting various charities there for years. It was part of our ministry and also our duty as overseas Indians."

The company in question was poised to expand its subscriber base by hundreds of thousands. As Rohit explained it, by investing, Naveen and Geeta would be buying a stake in his cousin's company and could expect a 20 to 25 percent rate of return within a year, paid in biannual installments. They didn't hesitate.

"We've known this boy all his life. We were at his baptism. His mother is my best friend. If he said it was a worthwhile opportunity, my husband and I were happy to become involved."

The Nairs wrote Rohit a check for $10,000. He then made the rounds of church members, who knew him and his family well. He managed to raise a total of $250,000.

"People at church were very interested in it. We were proud to see him doing something for his community and taking an entrepreneurial initiative. After he got the money, he flew back to India and we didn't hear anything for a while. He told us not to expect any news for a few months, so that was not unexpected."

Rohit had promised the Nairs their first dividend check by the end of the year. With Christmas approaching, they still had not seen Rohit. Then one Sunday, he made a surprise appearance at church.

"Even his parents didn't know he was due back in the country. Ashna said he had turned up suddenly without any notice. Anyway, we were all happy to see him, of course, and eager to hear any news of our enterprise."

All smiles, Rohit was full of good news for Geeta, Naveen, and the other investors. His cousin's firm had won some lucrative contracts and he had checks for them all.

The check was not as big as Naveen had expected. "It was only $250, but Rohit explained that a lot of the funds were still tied up in India. The company was in the middle of erecting mobile phone towers in very remote areas. He said they were busy negotiating with a European mobile phone manufacturer, and he gave my wife and me new phones that he said were samples of the kind that would be on offer to these new subscribers."

Geeta noted Rohit's new look. "His clothes were very expensive. His watch was a Rolex. My husband kept asking how much he had paid for it. His mother told me he had moved out of their home and was leasing an apartment but was often off traveling."

On one of his trips home, Rohit convinced the church's pastor to let him use the church hall for a presentation. Dozens of existing investors attended, along with prospective new investors. The pastor began the meeting by praying for the success of the business venture and announced that Rohit had pledged a donation to the church in the amount of $50,000. Attendees heard Rohit give an update on the project in India and listened to church members provide testimonials on the soundness of the endeavor.

"He asked how many people in the room had invested money with him," Naveen recounts. "About half raised their hands. He asked how many had been paid. The same people raised their hands, including us. It was a very effective demonstration. Many people were eager to join up."

Geeta adds, "I heard that he was visiting other Indian churches around the country and had managed to sign up investors everywhere he went."

The couple didn't hear much from Rohit after that, although they did receive a second dividend check, a month late. Again, it was for much less than expected.

"I was curious to know how things were going," says Naveen, "but it was difficult to get in touch with him. I would e-mail Rohit, and once in a while he would reply, but it was always very positive. Things are going great, money will be flowing soon. Any delays he always blamed on government bureaucracy or red tape."

A year after investing $10,000, Geeta and Naveen had received only $750 back. And they began to hear grumblings from other investors. "Friends of ours who had given Rohit money told us that they still had not received any dividends. They wondered if there were problems with the business. Then another friend returned from India, where he had made inquiries about Rohit's business venture. No one there had heard anything about it. They asked us to talk to his parents to see if we could get any more information. I told Naveen we had to do something."

Reluctantly, the couple paid a visit to Rohit's family. Ashna wept as she admitted to them that she had not seen or heard from her son in more than a month. His father, Joseph, was apologetic. Confiding in the Nairs, he told them that they too had invested a considerable sum. Initially, Rohit had come back with a sizeable check that he said was their first payout. Since then, they had received nothing. Finally, Joseph became concerned enough to contact relatives in India for more information.

"Then he just stopped talking. He couldn't look us in the eye," says Geeta. "I thought, my God, what is it?"

After a long pause, Joseph said that he had spoken to the cousin in question, the one with the telecommunications business. He remembered taking Rohit on a tour of his sites and said that Rohit had seemed very interested. The cousin had indeed asked Rohit if he wanted to invest in his business. But Rohit had declined, pleading poverty. As far as the cousin was concerned, that was the end of the episode.

Geeta and Naveen were dumbfounded. "We were very confused," says Naveen. "Rohit had obviously fabricated part of the story. Maybe the cousin was lying? Or was Rohit collecting money without the cousin knowing? If so, why? We had so many questions, but they had no answers. His parents were very upset, we could see, so we left."

It wasn't until they were back home that Geeta raised the question they had both been avoiding. Was Rohit a crook?

Naveen discounted the possibility at first. "It made no sense. He was from a good family. He grew up with our children and was like a son to us. He had a very good education. He was smart. Why would he do it? It must be some kind of misunderstanding, or someone must have misled him. That's what I thought."

But Geeta was not so sure. "His mother's face, I could tell she felt the same as I did. I said to Naveen, our money is gone. Rohit is gone. We argued about it, because he refused to accept it. But in the end, I'm sorry to say, I was right."

Because of their friendship with Rohit's parents, the Nairs decided against reporting the incident to the police. Other investors, however, were not so charitable. Multiple complaints were filed with the police, and a warrant was issued for Rohit's arrest. An investigation revealed that he had bilked investors nationwide of a total of $1.5 million. Instead of putting the money into telecommunications systems, he had pocketed it, buying himself luxury goods and paying for first-class travel to exotic destinations. By the time authorities came looking, he had gone into hiding. His victims assumed he was in India but out of reach.

"He would have to go somewhere far away from his family home. No one has seen or heard from him since then. Many people lost a lot of money, but it's his parents who have really suffered. They had to move away because of the shame. There were people who believed that they had something to do with it, or at least helped him escape. I don't think so myself," says Geeta, "but they lost all their friends. It was too painful."

Affinity fraud has been perpetrated against every group imaginable. Con artists peddling phony high-yield investments have targeted churchgoers in the rural Midwest, even going so far as to give their funds biblical names such as the Revelation Trust fund. Identifying themselves as born-again Christians, the scammers told potential investors that it was their religious duty to invest in the funds and recruited other church members to solicit on their behalf.

The "miracle cars" scam was another aimed at churchgoers. The original perpetrators told a congregation in California that several cars were being made available at low cost from the estate of a deceased millionaire. For a mere $1,000, parishioners could purchase a low-mileage, late-model car. The only hitch? Delivery would be delayed while the millionaire's will was processed in probate court. The vehicles came to be known as the "miracle cars," and word spread like wildfire from church to church across the country. A total of $20 million was collected for nonexistent cars. Along the way, antsy buyers who asked for refunds were reimbursed using money collected from other victims. It was the classic Ponzi setup.

Pyramid and Ponzi schemes flourish in religious populations, where people are presumed to possess a certain standard of morality. Some victims in the miracle car scam were approached by their own pastors or members of their congregation whom they had known and trusted for years. Certainly, the thinking went, these people would not swindle them.

But religious congregations are not the only places where affinity frauds exist. Ethnic groups are also popular with fraudsters. First-generation immigrants, particularly those who do not speak English as a first language, are especially susceptible to affinity fraud. Senior citizens and retirees are another common target.

Anytime people share a kinship, bond, or common experience, affinity fraud can strike. This includes alumni groups, parenting networks, social clubs, neighborhood associations, even the workplace. Affinity can be established and abused among coworkers. A Connecticut man told coworkers that he would be able to obtain tickets to a SuperBowl in Florida. Nineteen people paid out $150 per ticket and flew down to Florida, only to find that they had been duped. An Indiana factory worker bilked his coworkers of $160,000 to buy shares in companies that turned out to be fictional.

PROTECTING YOURSELF

There are plenty of legitimate business opportunities and legitimate investment opportunities. Separating the good from the bad should not be that difficult if you take your time and do your homework.

Look for warning signs. Pyramid schemes will have some or all of the following elements:

- High-pressure sales tactics.
- Commission for recruitment of new members.
- Sales not to the public, only to other participants.
- Promises of quick and large returns on your investment.
- Testimonials from individuals who claim to have had wild success with the program.
- No customer support.
- A complicated or vague investment process.

Ponzi schemes will often bear the following hallmarks:

- Absence of sound documentation and verification.
- Promises of quick and unusually large returns on your investment.
- Lack of fluctuation in investment performance.
- Difficulty in accessing your money or contacting the person at the top.

Do your research. The Securities and Exchange Commission website has information on how to check on investment advisers and brokers before investing your money. See www.sec.gov/investor/brokers.htm for tips and links to databases of licensed brokers as well as state regulatory agencies.

Dig for dirt. If you are looking to become involved in a business venture, check with the state attorney general's office and the Better Business Bureau to see if they have any information on the company. Depending on the organization's size and history, a simple Web search may also turn up complaints and news stories.

Read the fine print. If you are required to buy inventory, find out if there is a buyback or refund policy. Look into what kind of help the company provides in the way of marketing, advertising, and distribution. The last thing you want is to be stuck with a basement full of herbal supplements or cosmetics that you can't unload.

Educate yourself. Financial matters are by their nature complex. Take the time to understand what you're getting into. Many books written for the layperson explain the different kinds of investments and what to expect when you invest. Once you have invested your money, you should always be able to obtain information on the investment's performance and receive satisfactory answers to your questions.

Get it in writing. If investing in a business, get all terms and conditions in writing. Anything that you are told in person should be backed up by hard copy. Do not take anything for granted. If it's not written down, you have no proof that it was ever promised. If the document you are given looks like legalese, take it to an independent attorney and have it read through.

Do not sign anything without fully understanding your obligations and rights. If investing in a fund, ask for a prospectus. All legitimate investment funds are legally obligated to supply you with a prospectus that outlines the fund's investment objectives and past performance as well as risks and fees associated with the investment.

Resist the hard sell. Beware of anyone who attempts to pressure you into signing anything or handing over money on the spot. Successful pyramid con artists utilize high-pressure sales seminars to convince people to invest in their schemes. They will dazzle you with stories of how their product, service, or investment is such a hot item that it will have the money pouring in.

Do not put all your eggs in one basket. Whatever the amount, don't commit all or even a large chunk of your savings to just one investment. Even legitimate investments fail from time to time; illegitimate investments fail 100 percent of the time. When money managers talk about diversifying your portfolio, this is exactly what they mean. The amount is not important; what is important is what it represents to you and your financial security.

Trust no one. It doesn't matter if it's someone your brother has known all his life, a classmate, or a former babysitter. Shared experience or identity does not make a person trustworthy. Pyramid scheme operators rely on their victims to go first to those closest to them, their family and friends, so it is possible that the person soliciting you is not even aware that what they are involved in is a scam.

Do not rely on testimonials. Every pyramid and Ponzi scheme will have supporters whose job it is to rave about how it's going to change your life and land you on Easy Street. Often these "shills" are part of the racket themselves, especially if they appear in promotional videos. Or they may be victims too, hoping for a big score if they recruit you and others. Either way, if you start seeing pictures of mansions and yachts, run for your life. It's bound to be a scam.

Seek help soon. If you think you or someone you know has been targeted by a pyramid or Ponzi scheme, notify the authorities immediately. Contact your local police department. You can also file a complaint with the Federal Trade Commission (www.ftccomplaintassistant.gov) that will be entered into a database accessed by law enforcement personnel worldwide. Although there are exceptions, pyramid schemes are often short-lived, so the quicker you act, the quicker the authorities can shut the operation down and bring the perpetrators to justice.

(10)

IT AIN'T ME

Identity Theft

Nathan and Kelly use online banking to pay most of their bills, but there are still occasions when they pull out the checkbook, such as Kelly's niece's graduation. Kelly picked out a graduation card and decided to enclose a check with it.

"I decided against sending a gift card because you can feel a card inside an envelope. It's probably safer to send a check. Ironic, isn't it?"

With the envelope stamped and ready to go, Nathan was charged with dropping it off at the post office. In the rush of the morning commute, he forgot. Later, he came across the card in his bag at work and put it in the office mailbox.

About a week later, Kelly was checking her bank account and saw that the check had been cashed. "I thought, great, she got it. But I never heard anything from her, which was unusual. She's the type of person who's good about acknowledging gifts and sending out thank you cards. I mentioned it to my mother, and word must have filtered back to my niece, because then she called to say she'd never received the card."

Kelly was mystified. Then who had cashed the check? And how? She contacted the bank. "While I was on the phone with customer service, she asked me if I'd looked at the check online. It turns out that each check is scanned and the electronic scan is available to me on the website. I logged in, clicked on that check number, and it showed me the front of the check. My signature, the date, and the amount were all intact. But someone had gone in and changed the payee name to something else. It was hard to read, but the name looked like David Lewis or Loomis. It was really weird to see this check of mine, written by me, made out to someone I'd never heard of."

Kelly told the bank representative that the check had been altered. "I said, can't we track down this David Lewis, whoever he is? And she chuckled, like, oh sweetie, that's not his real name. Have you seen *The Bourne Identity*, where Matt Damon has all those fake passports? Apparently it's like that." Although it was too late to stop payment on the $100, the bank closed the account to prevent further fraud. "They were pretty much done with me after that," she said, "but I took it to the police too. I told Nathan somebody in his office building had probably swiped that mail and was continuing to do it."

The police officer taking Kelly's report told her that check forgery was very prevalent, but that few people bothered to report it. "He said that he saw a lot of check forgery being committed by meth addicts. They use some kind of solvent to wash the checks or remove the original payee's name. Sometimes they keep the check amount the same in order not to raise suspicion, but other times they erase all the information and write a completely new check. Or if they're really resourceful, they use that check to make a bunch of fake ones and start writing multiple checks on your account."

Nathan also reported the theft to his building's security team, which conducted its own investigation. "I think what they found out horrified them. My company occupies the whole building, so we have a central mailroom where the mail is sorted. It turns out that there was siphoning of both incoming and outgoing mail. When they looked through the dumpsters at the back of the building, they found boxes of bulk mail that had been tossed. They found confidential mail that had been opened. Total dysfunction. There was a criminal element, obviously, given our personal experience, but there was also an element of people trying to keep up with the sheer volume of work. The firm contracts with a third-party vendor for mail services. That contractor employs the mailroom staff. Their main focus is high performance and low cost, so the vetting of employees is not necessarily the most stringent. Meanwhile, they have really high standards for how much mail needs to be processed hourly and daily. And these people have free and easy access to all our mail. The conditions are perfect for identity theft."

It may surprise you to know just how many people would like to be you or at least spend money as you. Last year, more than 11 million Americans were victims of fraud due to identity theft. Identity theft is an equal opportunity crime. It can affect anyone and can occur almost anywhere—through the mail, over the phone, via e-mail, face to face, or even remotely. Specific forms of identity theft such as phishing and pretexting have already been touched on in previous chapters, but it's worth taking a look at the bigger picture, since identity theft is one of the most well-known and widespread forms of fraud in operation today.

According to the Federal Trade Commission (FTC), identity theft takes place when someone uses your personal information, such as a credit card number or a Social Security number, without permission, to commit fraud or other crimes. Credit card fraud is the most common form of reported identity theft, followed by phone or utilities fraud, employment fraud, and bank fraud. Identity thieves can set up new credit card, phone, and utility accounts using the names and personal information of their victims. They may also use existing accounts to pay for goods and services. Stolen identities are utilized to obtain loans, file fraudulent tax returns, forge documents, apply for government benefits, rent property, and do just about anything that requires a name, address, and Social Security number.

A WORLD OF HURT

Stealing someone's identity can be as simple as rifling through a co-worker's purse when she steps away from her desk. It can be a more organized effort to monitor postal routes and intercept mail. And it can be on a grand scale, as with data breaches affecting tens or hundreds of thousands of people at once. Health care facilities, credit card companies, retail outlets, universities, and government agencies are among the institutions that maintain large databases and are therefore fertile ground for identity thieves.

Alice's husband, Mitch, hates potlucks. "He usually only eats whatever I make, because he says that way he knows it's safe. But sometimes you have no choice." At a family Thanksgiving dinner, Mitch's sister dished up a plate of food for him, with a healthy serving of mashed potatoes and gravy. When he returned home several hours later, Mitch was beginning to feel the ill effects of potluck roulette. By the middle of the night, he was in agony. Alice drove him to hospital emergency room, where he was treated and sent home.

That short visit solved his immediate physical ailment, although he swore off potlucks forever. His long-term woes, however, were just beginning.

Three months after the hospital trip, strange things began happening. "First it was letters. I'd receive letters from debt collectors saying that I owed for this or that—credit cards, a car loan, even furniture. Then the calls started. They called day and night, not just Alice and me, but they started calling my relatives too. I couldn't figure out what was going on."

At first, Mitch answered the calls and patiently explained to the debt collectors that there must be some mistake; he hadn't spent the money in question. The callers refused to take no for an answer, and Mitch and Alice eventually stopped answering the phone.

"Our son Chris said they must have had Mitch confused with someone else who has the same name. He told Mitch to get a copy of his credit report so he could prove it wasn't him. Chris showed him how to do it. It was the first time he'd ever seen his credit report. It was a little spooky, all the information it had in it."

There, buried within a lifetime's worth of loans and accounts, were five new credit card accounts, all opened recently, and all overdue, with charges totaling more than $15,000.

Mitch was astounded. "It's hard to explain the feeling. It was more than a slap in the face. It was like someone had crawled under my skin. It gave me chills. I just didn't understand how this could have happened."

While he began the process of trying to sort out his finances and damaged credit, the harassing calls continued, with collectors threatening legal action. In the middle of this chaos, a letter from the hospital arrived.

They regretted to inform Mitch that they had experienced a serious data breach. A total of 50,000 patient files had been jeopardized, including his. The personal information he provided to the hospital was stolen by a disgruntled hospital employee and sold, along with the personal records of hundreds of other patients, to a ring of identity thieves. The thieves used the names, addresses, and Social Security numbers of their unsuspecting victims to open up new credit accounts, take out loans, and rack up millions of dollars of debt.

Like Mitch, many former hospital patients did not realize their identities had been stolen until they received calls from collection agencies demanding payment. He was shocked and devastated. "I guess what bothered me more than anything was that they would take advantage of folks in the hospital. I had gone there for help and I ended up with a world of hurt."

Unfortunately, data breaches are all too common within large organizations. However, there are steps you can take to minimize your risk of exposure. It is important to realize that identifying information, especially a Social Security number, does not have to be provided every time it is requested. In filling out forms, we are accustomed to seeing blanks for Social Security numbers. Many people assume that because the space is there, they have to fill it in. This is not true. An employer, a bank, the IRS—these are examples of organizations that require a Social Security number. A dentist's office, a grocery store, a utility company do not. Utility companies routinely ask for Social Security numbers in order to complete credit checks for new account holders, but according to the Social Security Administration, this is not strictly necessary. They can use other methods to run credit checks. Before you give your number, you may want to ask why it is needed, how it will be used, what law mandates its provision, and what will happen if you do not provide it. Alternatively, simply leave that space blank and see what happens.

SKIMMING OFF THE TOP

Perry, a public relations account manager in Chicago, received a long-awaited promotion at work and was eager to celebrate. He invited five close friends out for a night on the town, his treat.

"My friends joke that I'm kind of tight with money. They call me cheap, but I like to think of myself as economical. Either way, I'm not known for being a big spender. But this was a special occasion. I had been working really hard for the promotion, so I wanted to splash out a little, throw caution to the wind. We started off at a Spanish restaurant I'd been wanting to try."

The group lingered over a tableful of tapas and several bottles of *cava*, Spanish sparkling wine. "It was absolutely delicious," says Perry. "We didn't hold back."

After dinner, the friends went on to a small club for more drinks and a little dancing. Perry put all the evening's expenses on his credit card. "It's one of those cards where you get a point for every dollar you spend, so at the back of my mind, I was aware of the fact that even though I was spending money, I was also earning points."

A great time was had by all, and Perry enjoyed himself thoroughly. The following Monday, he went in to work and took up his new position. Apart from that, life went on as normal, until the end of the month.

"I got my credit card bill by e-mail. There was an astronomical balance on it. My card was maxed out. I have a high limit because I have a really good credit score. But even so, it was still maxed out."

Perry looked at the list of charges. In addition to those he had made himself, there were a dozen more, including charges for gift cards, meals, appliances, iPods, apparel, and other assorted goodies. He immediately called the credit card company.

Perry was not alone. Other credit card holders had been similarly victimized. The credit card company contacted the U.S. Secret Service. A subsequent investigation uncovered a skimming ring working out of the Spanish restaurant.

Skimming refers to stealing credit or debit card numbers while processing the card. This can occur at a restaurant, store, gas station, or anywhere else that a card transaction takes place, including an ATM. When the card is swiped, a con artist uses a skimmer, a portable card reader, to retrieve and store the card information electronically. The information can then be used to charge purchases to the victim's card.

Perry contested the charges with his credit card company. He suspected that the fraud was linked to his night out, because all the fraudulent purchases had been made after that date. However, he had no idea how sophisticated the scam really was. "I ended up reading all about it in the newspaper," says Perry.

The server, a woman Perry remembers as attentive and friendly, ran his card through a skimmer, as she had also done with the cards of more than 100 other patrons. The skimming machine was then passed on to an outside accomplice.

"These accomplices gave her a handheld machine to take into work. Apparently she was paid $30 for each card she skimmed. The guys she worked with used the skimmers to make duplicate cards and then returned the machines to her to reload. It was a neat little scheme she had going. The only problem was that each transaction was traceable back to her, and it must have quickly become obvious that all of the victims had eaten at the same place. Now I'm regretting giving her such a good tip."

Perry wonders what would have happened if he'd had different spending habits. "I always check my credit card statement very carefully because that's how I am. Also, I don't spend a lot of money, so it was pretty obvious that those charges were bogus. They really stood out. But if you are someone a little less careful, someone who is always whipping out that card, would you really notice a few extra charges? I know there are executives in my own company who travel overseas and regularly charge tens of thousands of dollars a month on their corporate cards. Those guys aren't going through their bills with a fine-tooth comb. In fact, I doubt whether they ever even look at them. They just have their assistants eyeball them and send them on for payment."

In Perry's case, the card had to be handed over to his server in order for information to be captured. He might have been able to prevent the skimming if he hadn't let the card out of his sight. Unfortunately, keeping a card in your possession does not eliminate the risk of theft. Skimming devices have been attached to gas pumps, ATMs, and other points of purchase, where they can be disguised as part of the machine or even installed within it. In other words, victims themselves can unknowingly put their card information into the wrong hands.

Spotting a skimming device can be difficult. Clumsy skimmers may be different in color from the rest of the machine, may not fit well, or may show signs of being affixed onto the machine (tape, wires, glue). High-quality skimmers, on the other hand, can be nearly identical to the original. Familiarizing yourself with the different parts of your ATM or gas pump will help you to spot anything out of the ordinary. Skimmers are also more likely to be placed in areas where tampering will go unnoticed. An ATM in a bank lobby is less likely to have a skimmer on it than an ATM at a shopping mall, for instance.

CASH FOR TRASH

On the other end of the technical spectrum, *dumpster diving* may sound like an odd way to make a buck, but the overhead is low. Believe it or not, thieves do sift through trash in search of statements, bills, invoices, pre-approved offers of credit, or any documents containing personal details. And now, thanks to recycling, they don't even have to wade through rotting food to get to that nice, clean paper.

With the information gained from your trash, identity thieves can forge documents, charge goods on your credit card, and open up new accounts in your name, all without your even realizing it. A Florida man was arrested for forging checks using information gained through dumpster diving and mailbox theft. Police said he was making up to $10,000 a week in the scam.

Jake, a single father, had no idea his identity had been compromised until he received a bill from the electric company with two months' worth of charges on it, plus a returned check fee. "I did a double take, because I've never had a check returned before. I called the electric company. They said the check had bounced. I called my bank. The bank said there wasn't enough money in my account to cover the check. That was impossible. There are times when my account gets low, but I'd just been paid. It didn't make sense."

Going over recent account activity with the bank, Jake discovered that nearly all the money in his savings account had been transferred to his checking account and subsequently withdrawn. "This is a problem for me. I've got bills coming due right and left. Then as I'm trying to sort it all out, the police show up at my house and they have copies of my driver's license with somebody else's face on it."

The police informed Jake that fake IDs with his name and address had been found in a house raided by police during a drug bust. Among the thousands of pieces of evidence confiscated during the raid were several pieces of mail addressed to Jake, including a bank account state-ment, a medical bill, and insurance papers.

"The police said the mail could have been intercepted at the post office or picked out of my mailbox. Just like that."

Jake was not alone; his information was found along with that of hundreds of other victims. Yet the theft felt very personal to him.

"The money they took, that was not just my money. That was money for the rent, for food, for gas. They took food out of my children's mouths."

Mailbox theft is essentially dumpster diving without the dumpster. If you stop receiving mail or are missing certain pieces of mail, you may be the victim of identity theft. Thieves can submit a change of address form to have mail redirected or may go directly to mailboxes and retrieve mail. That's how Kelly's graduation gift ended up being cashed by a complete stranger.

Bank and credit card statements aren't the only pieces of mail that are useful to criminals. Personal mail such as cards or letters will contain information that can be used to perpetrate different kinds of scams. In one case, a conner phoned the parents of a teenage girl to say she had been injured in a skiing accident in Colorado. To authorize treatment, they would need to provide her Social Security number. The caller sounded legitimate because he knew the daughter's name, where she was, and what she was doing. It was all information she had put in a postcard to her parents the week before.

JUST A PRETEXT

Tia and her boyfriend had returned from a two-week vacation to the Bahamas when she received an e-mail from the airline asking her to complete a survey about her trip. In return for participating, she would receive $50 and her name would go into a drawing for 100,000 free airline miles.

"I wasn't going to do it, but then I thought, why not? It would only take a few minutes. We'd had such an awesome time in the Bahamas, and if there was a chance of winning those miles and getting a free ticket somewhere, it seemed worth it."

The e-mail included a link that sent Tia to a Web page where she had to enter her name, frequent flyer number, and password. After she did, it prompted her to answer a few questions about the airline's service. On the final page, she was asked for her Social Security number and address in order to receive the $50 payment. The whole thing took under five minutes.

Tia had responded to a phishing e-mail, in which a phony story is concocted in order to persuade someone to hand over personal details. This can be anything from a fake bank alert to an urgent call about an injured loved one. In each case, the victim is asked to provide a credit card or Social Security number or bank account information. Phishing refers to the e-mail variety of this kind of scam. More generally, it is known as *pretexting*, where someone contacts you on a false pretext or premise and attempts to extract information.

On the phone, pretexting calls can be live or recorded. Callers claim to be from research companies, financial institutions, or other legitimate organizations and request your personal information or a call back. They may claim that there is an "urgent" need for you to call immediately. They may even tell you that you have won a prize of some kind in order to entice you into revealing personal details.

Phishing e-mails are more sophisticated. They usually contain links to websites designed to capture personal information. Alternatively, they include attachments that will launch a Trojan horse or spyware program on your computer system in order to retrieve stored passwords and account numbers. They can also detect if you access a bank's website, and they can replicate the site in order to capture the information you enter.

The message Tia received was sent out to members of a specific airline's mileage program, putting it in the category of spear phishing, a customized form of phishing that zeroes in on particular segments of the population. The e-mail also identified Tia as having traveled recently, making it likely that the senders had access to the airline's passenger database.

After filling out the survey, Tia promptly forgot about it. "My boyfriend pays the bills, and we had been expecting a big credit card bill that month because of our trip. Sure enough, it was a big one. He paid off the minimum balance, like we always do, and that was it."

Meanwhile, at the credit card company, a red flag had gone up.

Faith works in account security for a major credit card company. Although she did not work on Tia's case, the scenario is a familiar one to her. "Many of our clients don't even realize that fraud alerts are a service we offer until they get a call from us. We have ways of detecting irregular activity. It basically involves monitoring spending patterns, looking at dates, times, and locations of purchases. If a cardholder goes on an overseas trip and uses the card, that will warrant a second look, because he or she isn't spending money in the usual places. We want to make sure these transactions are legitimate."

In fact, Tia had already received a call from her credit card company, related to her purchases in the Bahamas. "When we got back, there was a message asking us to verify some charges that we'd made in Nassau. I called and told them it was fine. Then about a month later, there was another voicemail from the credit card company talking about verification again. That time I let it slide because I thought it was just more Bahamas stuff."

Another credit card bill arrived. Another payment was made. Luckily for Tia, her credit card company was persistent. They kept calling.

Faith elaborates. "If you live in, let's say, Boise, most of your purchases will probably appear as Boise purchases. Some may be to online retailers in other states. Then you take a trip to London and we see some transactions in London. Hotel, restaurants, souvenirs. We may call at this point to make sure it's really you. You say yes. Then you're back in Boise and your charges are domestic or local charges again. But then there's a charge in Moscow. And I'm not talking Moscow, Idaho. Immediately you get another call from us."

At her boyfriend's urging, Tia finally called the credit card company back. "They said charges had been made on my card in Shanghai, China. They wanted to know if I'd authorized the charges, and I said definitely not. I asked what the charges were for, and they said things like electronics, train tickets, clothes."

Tia had no idea how her card had been compromised until she received a second phishing e-mail. "In the middle of the whole credit card fiasco, I got another message asking me to participate in an airline survey. I thought it was a little weird, because it looked identical to the first one. So I called the airline and asked them about it. I was transferred to their IT department and they asked me to forward the e-mail. I did, right when I was on the phone with the guy. He told me that it was a hoax."

The airline representative warned Tia that any personal information she'd provided as part of the survey was now in the possession of criminals. "He advised me to contact my financial institutions. I told him I was way ahead of him. The deed was done. Chinese people dressed in designer clothing were playing Wii at that very moment, thanks to me. What made it extra annoying was when he told me that the airline does actually send out real surveys, but that this one just happened to be a fake."

DAYLIGHT ROBBERY

You're eating lunch in a food court with your bag safely at your side, wallet tucked inside. The zipper is closed. Halfway through your meal, you happen to look down. The wallet is now on top of your bag. There's something very wrong with this picture. Your heart starts beating a little faster as you slowly open the wallet. Driver's license, check. Insurance card, check. Credit card? Gone. Within minutes, thieves have hightailed to the camera store down the block and charged thousands of dollars of equipment to the card.

There are plenty of high-tech options available to identity thieves, but the most straightforward approaches are still the most popular. Whether in the form of a mugging or a theft of personal property from a home, workplace, or other location, robbery is perhaps the most low-tech form of identity theft. Identity thieves who steal from your person or home are looking for the same things as the dumpster diver, such as credit cards, checkbooks, and bank statements.

Depending on the level of their sophistication, they may actually steal the items, as during a mugging or pocket picking, or they may leave the items but steal the relevant information—numbers, dates of expiration—in order to delay your discovery of the theft. After all, if you find your credit card missing, you will call and cancel the card. But if your card is still in your wallet, you won't know you have been a victim until you receive your credit card bill.

This kind of theft can be premeditated or a crime of opportunity. Unfortunately for you, some of the most likely suspects are the people you know. How easy is it for coworkers, relatives, or acquaintances to lift something out of your wallet or sneak a couple of checks from your desk? Sometimes, as with Mitch at the hospital, people willingly hand over personal details for one purpose and end up being victimized when crooks utilize the information for their own gain.

Justine was a new mother when she attended a seminar for women interested in selling jewelry. "My son was a newborn and I was looking for something I could do as a sideline from home, not to make a fortune, but just to have some money coming in. One of my friends had been to a home party where a woman was showing a jewelry collection. She knows I've always had an interest in handcrafted jewelry and suggested I check it out. I did some research and found out that there was going to be an arts and crafts show in Cincinnati, which is about half an hour away."

Justine found a babysitter, printed out copies of her resume, and headed out to the show. "It was one of the first outings I'd had since my son was born, so I was quite excited. Plus, I love any kind of artsy stuff. There were tons of jewelry booths, so I just went along and talked to as many people as I could. Some of them were individuals starting out, trying to sell their own jewelry, but there were also some established companies represented. I got talking to a woman named Cherie at one booth. She was a little older, super friendly. The company she worked for specialized in jewelry with a vintage look, very beautiful. Cherie told me she had been working with them for three years."

Justine explained her interest in selling jewelry, prompting an enthusiastic response from Cherie. She told Justine about the many benefits of the job and encouraged her to pursue it.

"I gave her a copy of my resume and she gave me an application. I filled it out on the spot."

Justine considered the day a success. She had distributed all the copies of her resume and completed one job application. She returned home excited and optimistic.

"Of all the people I spoke to, Cherie was the one I connected with the most. That was also the company I was most interested in, and the one that seemed the most promising in terms of employment."

So when Justine didn't hear back from anyone, she was disappointed. "It was a bust. But I didn't give up. I found a list of jewelers who do direct sales and went through the list until I found one that was both a good fit and wanted me."

With her immediate career goals fulfilled, the arts and crafts show became a distant memory for Justine. She began hosting jewelry shows and enjoyed the social interaction as well as the selling. "I guess I never realized before that I have a talent for sales," she says. "I'm not shy about approaching people and pushing the product. The only problem is that I'm also my own best client. If I can just sell more than I buy, I'll be in good shape."

Meanwhile, Justine and her husband, Alfonso, had been house hunting and found a place they liked and could afford. They applied for a mortgage.

"We were looking forward to having a place of our own. The apartment was too small with the baby, and we were planning to have more kids. There was a lot of paperwork involved, but we got everything together and submitted it. It wasn't one of those crazy mortgages; it was completely within our means, and we had no concerns about qualifying for it."

Then the bank called with some bad news. Their application had been denied. "At first, I thought it was because of Al. I've always had good credit. But they said I was the one. They ran a credit check and I failed."

Confused, Justine requested a copy of her credit report. She found multiple fraudulent accounts, including utility accounts she had never opened and rent balances for places in which she had never lived. She went to the police.

"They traced it back through the apartment rentals to a woman. She had used various names, including mine, to rent different places for herself and family members. They were still trying to track down her real name, but they managed to find a photo of her. It was taken from a security camera, so it wasn't that clear. She looked familiar, but I couldn't place her right away. Then it just came to me. It was Cherie, the jewelry saleswoman."

Cherie had used the information on Justine's job application form, including her Social Security number, to do everyday things like rent an apartment, turn on the electricity, get cable TV, and buy a car. In the course of their investigation, police discovered that Cherie or someone in her family had also sold Justine's Social Security number to an undocumented immigrant, who used it to obtain a job.

"It was overwhelming," says Justine. "First of all, who does something like that? The whole time we're talking face to face, as I'm telling her about my newborn baby and how I'd like to make some extra cash, all she's thinking about is how she can steal from me. I find that unbelievable. Secondly, the problems it created for me, for us, were huge. Our whole mortgage situation was put on hold. We lost the house we wanted. I had to clear my credit history, which is still ongoing. There was the IRS to deal with, because somebody had been working on my Social Security number. Banks, credit card companies, utilities, police. It was a nightmare."

PROTECTING YOURSELF

Identity thieves are creative, seeking access by any means necessary. Mail, trash, and unattended bags are all sources of personal information. Skimming, phishing, and pretexting are used routinely to solicit and steal valuable details about individuals and their finances. Every two seconds, someone falls victim to identity theft. Most forms of identity theft are preventable, but protecting yourself requires changes in attitude and behavior.

Safeguarding your personal information and monitoring your finances are the keys to protecting yourself. A few simple steps can make all the difference.

Guard your mail. Invest in a locked mailbox. If you have anything to mail, take it directly to the post office rather than putting it in your home mailbox. If you are going out of town, put a hold on your mail. This can be done by filling out a form at your post office or online at www.usps.com. Held mail is available for delivery or pick up on your return.

Keep your numbers private. This includes your Social Security number, driver's license, passport, bank accounts, credit cards, retirement funds, PIN numbers, passwords, date of birth, even your address and phone number. Any piece of identification that is unique to you could help someone steal your identity and your assets.

Don't carry your Social Security card in your wallet. Keep it under lock and key. Don't give the number out unless absolutely necessary.

Many forms routinely ask for a Social Security number but do not require one. When in doubt, don't provide it, and see if they come back to you for it. If they do, ask why they need it. This is YOUR information. You are not obligated to share it with anyone if they cannot provide sufficient proof that they need it.

Secure all your private information. Don't leave your checkbook lying around in your car. Don't leave your wallet in an unlocked drawer at work. If you are in a public place, keep your bag, purse, or wallet zipped and close to you, preferably on your lap, not on the floor or on the back of a chair. You may think you live in a safe area or are surrounded by honest people, but a good rule of thumb is never to leave your personal belongings unattended unless you're willing to lose them. It only takes one set of sticky fingers to empty your bank account. This is not paranoia. This is caution.

Keep your eye on the card. To reduce the risk of skimming, use cash whenever you can, especially for small purchases. If you do use your credit or debit card, make sure you keep the card in sight. In a restaurant, you can ask to watch your card being swiped. This may feel awkward at first, but make it a habit and you'll get over that feeling soon enough. If you are withdrawing money from an ATM, make sure it is an ATM in a well-traveled, well-lit area, preferably in a bank lobby. Give the machine the once over before you use it. If anything looks unusual or haphazard, don't insert your card.

Shred private information. Personal shredders are inexpensive and easy to find. Even a basic $20 shredder will enable you to dispose of your personal documents safely. Shred anything that has identifying information on it. This includes your name and address. A note of warning: paper to be shredded accumulates more quickly than you would think, so daily shredding is a good idea. If you get to the point where the volume is more than you can handle personally, there is another solution. Many cities and towns host regular community shredding events where residents can bring in boxes of papers and other items to be shredded. Check with your local public works or environmental services department.

Be wary of e-mail. Immediately delete anything suspicious from an unknown source. Do not click on any links, even in e-mails that look like they're from trusted sources, unless you can independently verify their authenticity. *Do not* open attachments unless you are certain you know what they are and have scanned them for viruses. Unfortunately, scammers are able to hack into e-mail or social networking accounts and send out fraudulent messages that look like they're coming from friends. (See chapter 7.)

Monitor your bills and statements. Whether you receive them electronically or on paper, read each bill and statement carefully. If you see any charges or activity that you cannot account for, contact your bank or credit card company immediately. Many institutions will also contact you if they suspect a charge is fraudulent, but you shouldn't rely on them to do so.

Use online banking to keep an eye on your account. Review your bank account balances, withdrawals, and transfers. Check to ensure that charges are consistent with purchases that you have made. Look at checks paid on your account. Have they been tampered with? Are they made out to the right payee? It is especially important to monitor your bank accounts regularly, because under federal law your liability for unauthorized charges to your debit card is determined by the length of time between the charge and your reporting of it. The quicker you are able to notify the bank, the better.

Review your credit reports. You are legally entitled to a free copy of your credit report every 12 months. The three major consumer reporting agencies, Equifax, Experian, and TransUnion, have created a central website, www.annualcreditreport.com, where you can request your reports. You can also request them by phone at 1-877-322-8228.

To request the information by mail, you will first need to download and complete a request form that is available on the website. After completing the form, send it to: Annual Credit Report Request Service, P.O. Box 105281, Atlanta, GA 30348-5281.

Once you receive your credit report, look for any accounts that you have not opened yourself or any outstanding debts that do not look familiar.

(11)

RECOVERING FROM IDENTITY THEFT

Hanif lives in Michigan, but as an independent consultant, he travels frequently. A one-man operation, he makes all his own travel arrangements, usually sticking with the same hotel, airline, and rental car companies.

"I'm all over the place, so my credit card statements reflect that. I bill my clients for various expenses, so each month I go through my bills and identify which charges go with which client. One day I'm doing this, and I see a charge for a lingerie store in Tulsa. Oklahoma is one place I hadn't been recently, and a lingerie store, certainly not. I contacted my credit card company and let them know the charge was unauthorized. They said there had been several charges since then, and they went through them with me. Sure enough, whoever it was had made more charges to my card, all in the vicinity of Tulsa."

Taking the initiative, Hanif called the Tulsa police department and reported the credit card abuse. "They asked me if I'd done business with anyone in Tulsa in the past few weeks. I said no, not that I knew of. What was strange was that none of the charges were made in places that I'd actually visited, which made it seem like the card number hadn't been stolen anyplace I'd traveled. And the card itself was still in my possession."

So who or what was in Tulsa? Police had Hanif make a list of the companies to whom he'd provided his credit card number, whether in person, online, or on the phone, in the past two months. He placed a fraud alert on his credit report in order to prevent further abuse. His credit card company canceled the compromised card and sent him a new one.

"I never received the replacement card, and suddenly all my mail dried up. There was no mail arriving. Then I got one piece of mail, a confirmation of my change of address. Of course I hadn't submitted any change of address. The new address was a post office box in Tulsa, Oklahoma. So now this mystery person was having my mail forwarded and had probably received my new credit card."

Hanif gave the post office address to the police in Tulsa, but before they had time to check that lead, another one came through. He received a call from the detective he'd been working with. The suspect had been caught.

"He was in a car dealership, trying to buy a car. He had given them my information to run the credit check, but when it went through, the fraud alert came up, and the dealer contacted the police. When they showed up, he was still sitting in the salesman's office, negotiating a price."

The thief turned out to be a customer service representative at a Tulsa call center operated by Hanif's favorite rental car company. "From what they told me, he was just a young guy. They thought he'd probably targeted other customers too, but I was the only one who'd tried to track him down."

By acting quickly and contacting the police, Hanif was not only able to limit the damage done to his record but was also able to help police apprehend the perpetrator.

WHAT IF?

Hanif's case was unique for a couple of reasons. One is that he had the satisfaction of knowing that the perpetrator had been identified and apprehended. He was also very proactive in detecting and responding to the theft. Not all victims have the same opportunities or initiative.

Quick action is the key to recovery from financial identity theft. Unfortunately, it's not always possible. Unless you are the victim of a robbery and are able to react immediately, you may not even discover the identity theft until it has already occurred. If you are being vigilant, you will notice a discrepancy on one of your account statements. Otherwise, you may not realize you are a victim until your credit card is declined or you can't qualify for a loan despite your excellent credit history. If some of your mail goes missing, if you begin receiving unexpected calls from collection agencies—all these are signs that you may have been targeted by identity thieves.

Once the identity theft has been confirmed, anger and disbelief are understandable first reactions, followed by a feeling of being over-whelmed and helpless to correct the situation. It is difficult to believe that people make a full-time occupation of preying on others. Yet it is an unavoidable truth. For whatever reason, perhaps drugs, greed, laziness, or all of the above, these thieves operate by trading on your good name to obtain money, goods, or services. In the aftermath of identity theft, victims are left to pick up the pieces of their shattered finances, credit, and peace of mind.

Because identity theft is a broad category that encompasses a wide range of crimes, the recovery process will differ in length and complexity, depending on the exact nature of the theft, the amounts involved, and the timeline of events. It is important to remember, however, that recovery *is* possible, no matter how difficult the situation seems.

If identity theft does happen to you, do not panic. Help is available. The prevalence of identity theft means that financial institutions and law enforcement agencies are now familiar with the crime and have developed policies and procedures to deal with it. The following steps should be your first.

Close Your Accounts

Close any bank, credit card, or other accounts that you know have been accessed or any new accounts that have been opened in your name. You can assume that if one bank account has been compromised, they are all vulnerable, so close them all and start over. Dispute all fraudulent charges. Call the fraud department of each company imme-diately and follow up in writing, including copies of supporting docu-ments. The company will probably provide you with its own forms to complete. Make copies of all relevant paperwork.

Federal legislation offers protections for credit and debit card fraud, but you must act within a specified time frame in order to take advantage of them. For unauthorized ATM or debit card withdrawals, the quicker you act, the more money you will recoup. If you are able to notify your bank within two days of a fraudulent transaction, your liability will be limited to a maximum of $50. If you act within 60 days of the theft, that figure increases to $500. If more than 60 days elapses between the unauthorized charge and your notification, you may be liable for the entire amount. This applies to cases where your card has been physically stolen and also to instances in which the number and PIN have been appropriated, as in skimming or phishing.

With regard to credit cards, legally you cannot be held liable for more than $50 worth of fraudulent charges. Again, quick action is optimal. If your card is stolen and you are aware of the theft, call the credit card company immediately and they will cancel your card. If this happens in a timely manner, they will be able to flag any unauthorized charges that the thieves have made and remove them from your account. Alternatively, if you are scanning your monthly bill and notice something amiss, you can still start by contacting the credit card issuer by phone. Legally, however, you are required to submit a written letter disputing the fraudulent activity within 60 days in order to qualify for the liability protection. This means within 60 days of the date on the bill. Check with your individual credit card issuer to see what their specific requirements are, and do so sooner rather than later.

Place a Fraud Alert on Your Credit Report

Contact the three consumer reporting agencies to place a fraud alert on your credit report. A fraud alert informs creditors that they need to take added precautions before they open new accounts in your name or make changes to existing accounts. You only need to contact one of the companies, as they are legally required to contact the other two. However, you may want to follow up with the other two to ensure that they have been notified.

- **Equifax**
P.O. Box 740241
Atlanta, GA 30374-0241
Tel: 1-800-525-6285
www.equifax.com

- **Experian**
P.O. Box 9532
Allen, TX 75013
Tel: 1-888- 397-3742
www.experian.com

- **TransUnion Fraud Victim Assistance Division**
P.O. Box 6790
Fullerton, CA 92834-6790
Tel: 1-800-680-7289
www.transunion.com

To place a fraud alert, you will need to provide proof of your identity, which may include your Social Security number. Fraud alerts are either initial or extended. An *initial fraud alert* lasts for at least 90 days and is appropriate for those who have been identity theft victims or believe they are about to be victimized. An *extended alert* remains active for seven years and is for those who have already had their identities stolen. Unlike an initial alert, an extended alert requires potential creditors to contact you personally before issuing the credit.

Be aware that fraud alerts, while important, do not stop identity thieves from charging purchases to your existing accounts nor prevent them from opening accounts that do not require credit checks.

Request Copies of Your Credit Report

Once you place a fraud alert, you are able to request a free copy of your current credit report from all three agencies. Credit reports tend to be lengthy, since they contain all the debts you have incurred in the past as well as any current debt, including mortgages, student and auto loans, and credit cards. Read through the credit reports carefully and look for any discrepancies or unfamiliar debts, loans, or accounts. Check the balances of existing accounts to see if they are as expected.

The report will also contain information on how many inquiries have been made into your credit. This will give you an indication of how many times your credit file has been accessed by someone trying to set up accounts in your name. Credit reports can be illuminating even for those who have not been victimized by identity thieves. For those who have, it's not a pretty sight.

File a Police Report

File a police report and request a copy. This report is known as an identity theft report, and having one will enable you to exercise your rights under the Fair Credit Reporting Act. It may be required by creditors in order to recover your losses and will also be requested by the three credit reporting agencies if you are seeking to block fraudulent activity from appearing on your credit report. If you request an extended fraud alert on your credit report, you will have to provide an identity theft report filed with the local police or other law enforcement.

Contact the FTC

File a complaint with the Federal Trade Commission at www.ftc-complaintassistant.gov or by calling 1-877-ID-THEFT (438-4338). The more information the FTC has on identity theft and other forms of fraud, the better able it will be to help inform and protect consumers. The FTC will share the information with law enforcement agencies.

The FTC provides an identity theft affidavit form that can be used to notify financial institutions and creditors that you have been a victim of identity theft. The form should also be available through the police department.

Document Every Step

As soon as you discover the identity theft, start keeping a written record of the fraud you uncover and your subsequent actions. Whenever you contact someone by phone, take notes, get the individual's name, and log the date of the call. Send documents and letters via certified mail with a return receipt request. That way you have confirmation that they received the mail. Keep copies of any correspondence you send out or receive via hard copy or e-mail. A careful record of all transactions and communications will help to keep the process running smoothly and will ensure that you have access to whatever documents you need at any time.

The three main pieces of paper you will need to compile and keep together are the police report, a notarized identity theft affidavit report, and a cover letter summarizing your case.

Links to all these resources are available online at www.scamfu.com.

THE ID THEFT INDUSTRY

Following the laws of supply and demand, a number of companies now offer services and products designed to protect consumers from identity theft. It is likely that your bank and credit card companies offer their own forms of added protection. In some cases, the services offered are things that you can do yourself for free.

Companies may offer to block or freeze your credit, for a fee. This refers to blocking access to your credit report so that no one else can obtain credit in your name. States have different policies on credit freezing. Some allow all consumers to freeze their credit; others offer it only to those who have been victims of identity theft. See appendix B for information on how to obtain the information for your state. Remember that you are entitled to freeze your credit yourself at no charge if you have been victimized. If you are freezing your credit as a precautionary measure, you will be required to pay.

A credit or security freeze means that new creditors and third parties are denied access to your credit report, making it difficult for identity thieves to open new accounts in your name. Existing creditors and their collection agencies will continue to have access, meaning that your existing credit cards and bank accounts are still at risk. If you intend to apply for a new loan or some other form of credit while a freeze is in place, you will need to lift it temporarily using a PIN or password provided by the credit agencies. Lifting the freeze also involves paying a fee. To freeze your credit, you will need to contact each of the three credit bureaus and submit the required documentation and fees.

Other companies offer credit-monitoring services, which keep an eye on your accounts and alert you to any new accounts opened or inquiries made. This is not designed to prevent identity theft. By the time you are alerted, the theft may have already occurred. It is not foolproof. The monitoring does not necessarily account for new activity in existing unused accounts. It also may not cover all three credit bureaus.

Helping you rebuild your financial record after having your identity stolen can be a time-consuming and labor-intensive process, and there are companies that will assist you with it, for a price. This can involve obtaining a limited power of attorney to act on your behalf for the duration of the process. However, some institutions and law enforcement agencies will deal only with the victim and not a representative.

Consumers can also purchase identity theft insurance, but it's important to read the fine print. Insurance will not cover losses that result directly from the identity theft, but it may cover some the cost of rebuilding your identity, such as the cost of phone calls, photocopying, and mailing documents. These policies do not compensate you for the time you take off work to deal with identity theft issues, and in many cases they do not cover any legal fees you may incur. Identity theft insurance deductibles vary; some may be higher than the actual cost of recovering your identity. Many identity theft insurance policies will not cover you if a family member committed the theft, which is unfortunately more common than you would like to think.

Before signing up for or purchasing any products or services, do your research. Check with your credit card companies and banks to see what services they already offer for free. Most credit card companies offer some form of monitoring service and will contact you if they notice a charge that looks suspicious or questionable. Credit monitoring is also something that you can and should do yourself, even after you have resolved the immediate problems created by identity theft. By requesting copies of your credit report from the three major consumer reporting agencies, you can continue to monitor the activity on existing accounts as well as check for new, unauthorized accounts. Because there are three agencies and you are entitled to a free credit report from each one every 12 months, you can rotate agencies and check at least one report every 4 months.

UNDER THE RADAR

As a law enforcement officer, Raymond has had to be the bearer of bad news on more than one occasion. "The people who get burned especially badly are those who are in the dark about their finances. They've never seen their credit report, they don't look at bank statements, don't double check credit card bills. It's hard to believe, but there are people who have no idea what their bank balance should be; they go by what their ATM receipts tell them. Crooks will exploit this lack of oversight in order to maximize their profits."

To illustrate his point, Raymond shared the story of Wes, a 20-year-old college student. As a freshman, Wes opened a checking account at the credit union on campus. Like most college students, he was inundated with credit card offers as soon as he enrolled. He filled out applications for four or five—he can't recall the exact number—but only received two cards in the mail. He figured he wasn't approved for the others. Every month, his parents sent him a stipend check, which he deposited into the credit union account. Aside from the monthly deposits, he never went to the bank or checked his bank balance. He put all his expenses on his credit cards, occasionally withdrawing small amounts of spending money from the ATM.

The year went by with no sign of anything untoward. For his sophomore year, Wes, who had lived in a dorm as a freshman, made arrangements to rent a house off campus with a few friends. The four of them completed the rental application and returned to their respective homes for the summer. Just before the fall semester was due to begin, the landlord contacted Wes to say that his friends had passed the credit check but that he had not.

Wes didn't know what to make of this news. At his age, he had a scant credit history. Apart from student loans and the credit cards, he had no debt or assets. When he told his parents, they too were confused. They asked if he'd been paying his credit card bills on time. He said he had.

Wes and his father went online to check his credit report. Neither one had ever seen a credit report before. When they printed it out, the pile of paper was so thick that they couldn't staple it. In addition to the two credit card accounts Wes had legitimately opened, the report contained a dozen more accounts and loans taken out in his name, all in default or delinquent. The fraud dated back over several months, to the beginning of the academic year. But they were all new accounts, so his legitimate existing accounts remained untouched.

"Wes was lucky in one sense," says Raymond. "Because of his age, his life wasn't as complicated as that of someone twice his age. He didn't have a mortgage, a job, or a car. He only had the one bank account. He also had more free time than the average adult to dedicate to taking care of it. On the other hand, it was kind of a harsh introduction to life as an adult."

Wes began to take steps to repair his record. At his parents' urging, he went to the police and filed a report. Using the identity theft report, he was able to contact the credit agencies and have the fraudulent information removed from his record. Because his two legitimate credit card accounts had not been charged, he had no charges to dispute there, although he did replace both cards just to be safe. As an identity theft victim, he was able to institute a credit freeze at no cost.

The second victim Raymond cites is Nicola, a successful real estate agent in her early 40s. "At the time I met her, she and her husband had been married 20 years. The husband, Glenn, was an entrepreneur. He'd started off as a caddy at a country club and worked his way up to a management position. After a while, he decided he wanted to go into the restaurant business. Through his contacts at the club, he was able to find investors to back him, and he was off and running. That's how he met his wife. She and her girlfriends used to come into the restaurant and he wooed her."

Fast forward a couple of decades. Glenn owned a string of restaurants in South Florida. Nicola made a good living selling luxury homes. They had a daughter in high school. They vacationed in the Caribbean. From all outward appearances, they were living the American dream.

One day when Glenn was on a fishing trip in the Keys, Nicola got a call from one of the restaurant managers. A pipe had burst in the restaurant's restroom. He asked if Nicola could come and take a look at it. Nicola grabbed Glenn's keys and went down there. The restroom was flooded, and the manager was on the line with the insurance company. Nicola unlocked Glenn's office to see if any water had seeped in there. The floor was wet, but there didn't seem to be any major damage. "She started looking through the drawers and filing cabinets to see if she could find a copy of the insurance policy," Raymond recounted. "As she was doing so, she found a drawer that was so full, she could hardly open it. She finally wrenched it open. And it was like Pandora's box."

The drawer that Nicola had stumbled upon contained hundreds of unopened credit card bills. The bills, from a variety of credit card companies, were all addressed to Nicola. She began opening the envelopes and found thousands of dollars' worth of charges on each bill. Almost all of them were past due, with astronomical late fees and interest charges assessed. As Nicola related to Raymond much later, she began hyperventilating.

"She said she was looking at this paper in her hands, but she just couldn't accept what it meant. She immediately started rationalizing. Some employee must have done this, whatever this was, and Glenn had caught wind of it and confiscated the bills. But every time she ran a theory through her head, it hit a dead end. The bills were addressed to her at her *home*. There was no way they could have been intercepted by anyone at the restaurant. She decided she couldn't sort it all out right there and then, so she gathered all the envelopes together and took them home with her."

At home, she went through all the bills and began sorting them into groups to see how many cards they represented. She ended up with 12 piles. Then she started going through the piles and realized that within each one were different cards from the same issuer, so she had to make more stacks, each with a separate card number. "She wound up with 17 cards, all in her name. Then she began to add up the balances. It came out somewhere in the neighborhood of $240,000. So her husband had 17 credit cards or maybe even more, issued in her name, and had racked up nearly a quarter of a million dollars in debt. What was he buying? Her last hope was that he had spent the money on equipment and supplies for his restaurant. Not that that would make it all okay, but at least it would soften the blow a little. But it wasn't to be."

The charges were for personal items, meals, accommodations, and flights to places Nicola didn't know he had visited. Worse, there were charges to high-end jewelry stores, for floral deliveries, and for furnishings and electronics that Nicola knew were not in her own house, all indications that there was another woman in the picture and possibly even another home.

"It was a lot of earth-shattering information to process in a short amount of time. She didn't want to do anything rash. Glenn was due back a couple of days later. She wanted to confront him and hear what he had to say for himself. So she sat on it. Tough lady. When he finally returned, she hit him with it. He denied everything. Flat out denied it. He said one of his employees must have done it and planted the evidence in his desk. He claimed he hardly ever spent any time in that office. It would have been easy for someone to put the bills there. His tactic was, look, honey, I'm a victim too; I could never do something like this to you."

As Raymond described it, "At first she didn't buy it, but they had a lot of history and it was emotional and they were both crying. It went on for hours and then finally they were so exhausted they agreed to sleep on it. The next morning, she woke up and there was a note in the kitchen from Glenn. He said he'd gone to the restaurant to check on the water damage, he would be back by lunch. And that's the last she heard from him. He vanished completely."

After Glenn's disappearance, Nicola began to uncover more of the ugly truth. The restaurants were failing and headed into bankruptcy. Large sums of money had been withdrawn from the couple's joint bank accounts.

Nicola reported Glenn's multiple crimes to the police. When she began to tackle the credit card debt, she had a difficult time trying to convince the card issuers that the debt was not hers, a crucial step in having the charges removed from her credit report. Some of the companies she contacted told her that as a spouse, she was liable for her husband's charges. Repeatedly she was offered an opportunity to pay off the debt over time through a payment plan. She always refused.

"It's one thing to say that a total stranger halfway around the world has stolen your credit card number and abused it," Raymond points out. "It's far more difficult to convince creditors that you were completely unaware of the fraud when it's perpetrated by someone close to you in your own home. In certain cases, the credit card companies are justified. There are people who use identity theft as a ploy to try and write off some of their own debt. Of course, the creditors want to get paid, so if they can get you to agree to pay back some of it, they will. This may work with some people, especially those who feel bad for the family member or friend in question."

Identity theft by a family member, though quite common, can be a gray area. When a father gives his daughter his debit card and PIN number and she withdraws more than he has given permission for, is that identity theft? Is it identity theft when a husband uses a wife's credit card to order something without her consent? What if it happens on numerous occasions? Individuals must use their best judgment, but be aware that you are responsible for protecting your valuables, including personal information, to the best of your ability. Giving someone your PIN number can be construed as consent to make a withdrawal, making you liable for any losses. If your sister has a drinking problem and you've lent her your credit card and she abuses it, it's going to be tricky to explain to the credit card company that you don't want to pay for her bar tab.

In Nicola's case, the fraud was obviously perpetrated without her knowledge. The scale of it and the fact that she went to the police immediately after Glenn disappeared, made a formal report, and consistently disavowed any knowledge of his activities made her case easier to argue with the creditors. She was able to clear her credit history, but she was forced to declare bankruptcy because she was listed as coowner of the restaurants, all of which eventually closed. Nicola and her daughter lost their house. As for Glenn, police tracked him to Mexico, where the trail went cold. Their investigation determined that he had indeed been keeping another home, also in Florida. When they visited the home looking for him, they found his mistress, who was as much in the dark as Nicola had been. They advised her to check her credit report.

IN SICKNESS AND IN HEALTH

Stealing someone's identity in order to access a bank account or obtain a credit card is egregious enough, but an even more ominous form of identity theft involves the theft of an identity in order to access health care. Medical identity theft, in which a person's name, Social Security number, and other identifiers are stolen in order to receive free medical care, prescriptions, or other health-related goods or services can be not only financially devastating but also potentially dangerous. Important medical information such as surgical history, allergies, blood type, and medical conditions that are unique to one person are vital in determining and carrying out treatment and prescribing medications.

Medical identity theft can take place within a health care setting, when someone with access to medical records uses those records for a criminal purpose or when the office or institution suffers a data breach and someone working externally lifts the records. In these cases, the stolen information could be extensive and include medical history and insurance details, along with personal identifying information. It can also be a simple matter of an individual posing as someone else when enrolling for medical services, in which case the imposter might have only a few of the victim's details.

Victims discover they have been victims of medical identity theft in a variety of ways. The most shocking perhaps is when they receive a bill from a provider for medical services they never received. In the same vein, they may be contacted by collection agencies for unpaid medical bills they know nothing about. Insurance companies may refuse payment or deny coverage based on inaccurate information. Medical debts can also show up on credit reports. As with all forms of identity theft or fraud, victims should file a police report as soon as they discover they have been targeted.

Because medical records include identifying information such as Social Security numbers and dates of birth, victims may also want to utilize the same tools available to other identity theft victims, such as initiating a fraud alert or security freeze, which would limit further damage to their credit histories.

Under the Health Insurance Portability and Accountability Act (HIPAA), which governs the handling and disclosure of personal health information, patients have the right to request and receive a copy of their medical records, although the provider can assess a fee for the service. If the information in the records is incorrect, patients have the right to fix it. To make corrections, patients must submit them in writing to the insurance company and/or health care provider.

Unlike the credit bureaus, there is no central clearinghouse for health information. Those who want or need to review their medical records for inaccuracies must contact each individual health care provider with whom they do business. This includes hospitals and primary care physicians, but also emergency care clinics, pharmacies, labs, and testing facilities.

Navigating the red tape of hospitals and insurance companies is not always as straightforward as it ought to be. Victims can sometimes find it difficult to prove that they are who they say they are after an imposter has come in and filled out forms with alternative signatures and medical history. One man billed for an amputation had to show up in person to prove he could not be the patient in question because he still had all his limbs. Even so, when he went in for a preoperation screening months later, the nurse asked him about his dramatic weight loss. He had no idea what she meant until she told him that his last recorded weight—in other words, the imposter's weight—was 120 pounds heavier.

SOCIAL SECURITY

The original purpose of Social Security cards was to provide a way to link individuals with their Social Security benefits, accrued over a lifetime of work. Although they still have a role in employment, Social Security numbers have taken on a much larger significance. They are now a catch-all form of identification, used for everything from utility accounts to loan applications to student records. Unlike addresses or phone numbers, our Social Security numbers never change. They can unlock a treasure trove of goods and services such as bank accounts, credit cards, insurance, health care, federal benefits, and employment. Unfortunately, these same goods and services can become available to criminals at our expense if our precious numbers fall into the wrong hands.

Once a Social Security card has been compromised and identity theft takes place, it may be tempting to start over again with an entirely new Social Security number. However, this may not be as easy or as desirable as it may sound and is considered a last resort. It is possible to obtain a new Social Security number, but you will need to provide proof of your age, identity, citizenship, or lawful immigration status. More importantly, you will need to demonstrate that you are still experiencing problems due to the misuse of your number. According to the Social Security Administration, your problems may not end with the issuing of a new card, as all your records are linked to your old number and will need to be amended. Your tainted credit history may also remain associated with you through your name and address, which are unchanged.

A FINAL WORD

Recovery from the emotional and psychological impacts of identity theft may take longer than financial recovery. For one victim, Bonnie, the experience led to recurring nightmares in which she would open her wallet to find her credit cards and driver's license missing. Every time she had the nightmare, she awoke with a feeling of panic. She found herself opening her wallet at random moments during the day, obsessively checking each card to make sure it was still there. The feeling of anxiety persisted.

This is understandable. Identity theft is invasive and insidious. The theft feels intensely personal, even if the victim has had no contact with the thief. As with any crime, it is deeply disturbing to discover that there are those who make a regular occupation out of preying on innocent people. If there is any good to be extracted from the experience, it is that you have survived and things will improve. Having gone through all the steps to recover your financial security, you are now familiar with the various forms of protection that exist. Over time, Bonnie's recurrent nightmares tapered off, and she became a strong privacy advocate. She guards her personal information closely and is cautious in all her communications and online activities. Gradually, her feelings of anxiety diminished as she realized that although she could not guarantee that she would not be targeted again, she should at least do all she could to prevent it.

The best defense is always a thorough defense. It is crucial to monitor your credit report and all existing accounts in your name. Look for anything out of the ordinary. Treat any unsolicited contacts as potentially suspect and never, under any circumstances, give your personal information to anyone unless you have verified their identity independently. Be alert, aware, and cautious. You don't need to be paranoid; just be smart. By following the precautions in this book, you will lessen your risk of identity theft and all forms of fraud.

It's not possible to eliminate risk completely, and even the most careful people can become victims. The important thing to remember if you become a victim is to take action right away. The more time that elapses, the more damage an identity thief can do to your credit and finances. Knowing what steps to take will help you to act quickly. Identity theft is unfortunate and upsetting, but it is a fact of life. The best thing you can do is to educate yourself so that you are well armed and well prepared.

TAKEAWAY TIPS

TOP 10 WARNING SIGNS OF A CON

- High-pressure sales tactics.
- Need to act quickly.
- Need to keep it a secret.
- Request to wire money.
- Overpayment for goods or services.
- Request for personal information.
- Something offered to you by a stranger.
- Promise of quick and large returns on your investment.
- You've won!
- Absence of sound documentation and verification.

TOP 10 WAYS TO PROTECT YOURSELF

- Shred.
- Don't give out personal information.
- Put up a "no soliciting" sign.
- Secure your incoming and outgoing mail.
- Don't reply to unsolicited messages (e-mail *and* phone).

- Get on the Do Not Call Registry.
- Don't believe the hype; do your research.
- Verify identities and stories before acting.
- Keep personal documents under lock and key.
- If you suspect fraud, contact the police.

Carefulness can go everywhere.
—Chinese proverb

Ⓑ

RESOURCES

Web addresses constantly change. Check www.scamfu.com for the most current list of online resources.

GOVERNMENT AGENCIES

Attorneys General (by state)
Among other things, the state attorneys general act as public advocates for consumers. Through their offices of consumer affairs, they alert the public to fraudulent activity.
www.naag.org/attorneys_general.php

Consumer Protection Offices
(state, county and city governments)
www.consumeraction.gov/state.shtml

Federal Bureau of Investigation
The FBI maintains a useful list of common fraud schemes.
www.fbi.gov/majcases/fraud/fraudschemes.htm

Federal Communications Commission

The FCC is charged with regulating interstate and international communications by radio, television, wire, satellite, and cable. The FCC also has information on telephone, cell phone, and fax scams.
www.fcc.gov
1-888-CALL-FCC

Federal Trade Commission

The FTC is the nation's consumer protection agency and provides a wealth of information on scams and how to protect yourself.
www.ftc.gov
1-877-FTC-HELP

Postal Inspection Service

The Postal Inspection Service is charged with protecting the U.S. Postal Service, securing the nation's mail system, and ensuring public trust in the mail. They fight mail fraud.
http://postalinspectors.uspis.gov
1-877-876-2455

Securities and Exchange Commission (SEC)

The SEC's mission includes protecting investors from fraudulent investments.
www.sec.gov

If you are looking to invest, the SEC's tips on choosing brokers and investment advisers will be helpful.
www.sec.gov/investor/brokers.htm

SEC Toll-Free Investor Information Service.
1-800-SEC-0330

SPECIFIC TYPES OF FRAUD

FTC Identity Theft Site

The FTC offers a comprehensive guide to detecting and avoiding identity theft.
www.ftc.gov/idtheft

FTC Spam Site
http://www.ftc.gov/spam

Financial Fraud Enforcement Task Force
The task force was established in 2009 to hold accountable those who helped bring about the last financial crisis and to prevent another crisis from happening. There is a link on the site to report instances of fraud.
http://www.stopfraud.gov

CONSUMER ORGANIZATIONS

AARP
The AARP organization is intended for those 50 and over, but it offers handy information for people of all ages.
www.aarp.org/money/consumer

Better Business Bureau
The BBB aims to be "the leader in advancing marketplace trust," which means that they help consumers avoid fraud and find legitimate businesses.
www.bbb.org/us
1-703-276-0100

Coalition Against Insurance Fraud
The group acts as an anti-fraud watchdog geared specifically to the insurance industry.
www.insurancefraud.org

Identity Theft Resource Center
This nonprofit organization is dedicated to the understanding and prevention of identity theft.
www.idtheftcenter.org

National Consumer League
The nation's oldest consumer organization has two very good sites providing information on all kinds of scams. The fake checks site is packed with information on scams that use phony checks.

www.fraud.org
www.fakechecks.org
1-800-876-7060

Privacy Rights Clearinghouse
This nonprofit consumer organization focuses on the protection of personal privacy rights.
www.privacyrights.org
1-619-298-3396

FILING COMPLAINTS

FCC Consumer Complaints (phone/fax)
http://esupport.fcc.gov/complaints.htm

FTC
https://www.ftccomplaintassistant.gov

Financial Fraud
www.stopfraud.gov/report.html

Internet Crime Complaint Center
www.ic3.gov/default.aspx

U.S. Postal Inspection Service
https://postalinspectors.uspis.gov/contactUs/filecomplaint.aspx

TOOLS

Consumers Union
Guide to Security Freeze Protection
The nonprofit publishers of *Consumer Reports* offer a state-by-state guide to freezing your credit file.
www.defendyourdollars.org/2008/06/cus_guide_to_security_freeze_p
.html

Credit Report Request
For a free annual copy of your credit report.
https://www.annualcreditreport.com
1-877-322-8228

To obtain a copy by mail, you will need to download a request form from the site and send the completed form to:

Annual Credit Report Request Service
P.O. Box 105281
Atlanta, GA 30348-5281

Direct Marketing Association
Using the DMA's online tool, you can manage your direct mail preferences and cut down on the amount of junk mail you receive.
https://www.dmachoice.org

National Do Not Call Registry
https://www.donotcall.gov

ELECTRONIC SCAMS INFORMATION

Craigslist
www.craigslist.org/about/scams

EBay
http://pages.ebay.com/securitycenter/index.html

Microsoft
Microsoft's online safety and privacy education site includes good information on navigating safely online and creating secure passwords. Microsoft users can access the latest security updates.
www.microsoft.com/protect/default.aspx

PayPal Security Center
https://www.paypal.com/cgi-bin/webscr?cmd=_security-center-outside

STUDIES

FTC Consumer Fraud Survey
www.ftc.gov/opa/2007/10/fraud.pdf

Internet Crime Complaint Center (IC3)
The IC3 is a joint operation between the FBI and the National White Collar Crime Center. IC3 releases an annual report on cybercrime that provides national statistics as well as state-by-state figures.
www.ic3.gov/media/annualreports.aspx

Javelin Strategy and Research
Javelin produces an annual report on consumer identity fraud. A free consumer version is available for download.
www.idsafety.net/report.php

Ponemon Institute
The institute conducts independent research on privacy, data protection, and information security policy.
www.ponemon.org/research-studies-white-papers
www.ponemon.org/data-security

INDEX

credit repair scams, 37

credit report: blocking access to, 183; monitoring, 14, 185, 190, 192; placing fraud alert on, 180–82, 190; requesting copies, 175, 181–82, 184, 199

credit (security) freeze, 183, 190, 198

credit unions. *See* banks

crimeware kit (software), 103–6

crisis phone calls, 85–90

current events, 30

cybercrime, 5, 103, 200. *See also* electronic scams

data breaches, 161–63

data entry job scam, 53

date of birth. *See* birth date

dating, online, 38, 115, 118. *See also* sweetheart scams

Davis, Earl, 7–8

debit card fraud, 5, 94, 164, 174–75

debt collection cons, 91–92

debt reduction scams, 5; interest-rate reduction, 95–96

decennial census. *See* census

Direct Marketing Association, 199

disillusion/discovery phase, 28–31

donations, requests for, 79–81, 83. *See also* charity cons

Do Not Call Registry, 96, 101, 194, 199

door-to-door scams, 65–83; charity scammers, 79–81, 83; contracting scams, 65–75; effectiveness of, 74; protecting yourself, 81–83; ruse entry burglary, 75–76; salespeople, dishonest, 76–78

driver's license, 114, 166, 173

driveway repaving scam, 74

dumpster diving, 166–67, 170

DVD/movie clubs (negative options), 59–60

EBay, 199. *See also* auctions, online

economic crisis (recession), 4–5, 21, 30

the elderly. *See* senior citizens; *specific topics*

electronic (Internet) scams, 5, 103–21, 199–200; classified (online) ads, 108–11; cybercrime, 5, 103, 200; information, 199; Internet Crime Complaint Center (IC3), 5, 198, 200; malicious software, 61, 103–6, 168; Microsoft safety/education site, 199; the Nigerian scam, 118–19; pets, lost/missing, 111–13; protecting yourself, 61, 119–21, 175. *See also specific topics*, e.g., phishing; social networking sites; sweetheart scams

electronics "excess inventory" scams, 129–31, 138

e-mail, 5, 61; attachments, 168, 175; unsolicited, 119–20, 193. *See also* electronic scams; *specific topics*, e.g., phishing

emotions, manipulation of, 30, 35–39, 41–42, 44–45

employment scams/fraud, 5, 37, 93–94, 96, 161

envelope stuffing job scam, 53

Equifax. *See* consumer reporting agencies

escrow sites, online, 111

ethnic groups, 146, 155

European lottery. *See* foreign lotteries, fake

Experian. *See* consumer reporting agencies

ABOUT THE AUTHORS

James Munton, a successful magician, is an expert in deception and misdirection. He provides entertainment, marketing information, and training for corporations and organizations and has performed at the White House. An in-demand speaker on the subjects of identity theft and data breaches, Munton has appeared on various television news and information programs and in a National Geographic television documentary. He has been featured in articles in the *Washington Post* and *Wall Street Journal*. He is a past president of the National Capital chapters of both the International Brotherhood of Magicians and the Society of American Magicians.

Jelita McLeod, an award-winning writer, has worked in marketing, advocacy, and public relations for more than a decade. Her work has appeared in numerous publications, including the *Washington Post*, *Baltimore Sun*, *International Educator*, *College Board Review*, and *Vital Speeches of the Day*. Her commentary has aired on the National Public Radio program *All Things Considered*. McLeod has also served as a speechwriter and as director of external relations at the Fulbright Association. She has worked at the British Embassy in Washington, D.C., at Georgetown University, and in England and Japan.